reconcile

"John Paul Lederach calls each of us to peacemaking that is active, practical, and redemptive. He effectively demonstrates that reconciliation is not passive or optional in the life of believers."
—*Dale Hanson Bourke, author of* The Israeli-Palestinian Conflict

"A profoundly moving and inspiring book! John Paul Lederach's call to dream boldly and to act with enthusiastic pragmatism merits being taken seriously by pastors, students, and practitioners in the field."
—*Piet Meiring, former member of the South African Truth and Reconciliation Commission*

"As more Christians become aware and engaged in global conflicts, it becomes easy to choose sides. This timely book by Lederach reminds us that our call is to transcend conflict and bring transformation and reconciliation to all those involved."
—*Sami Awad, founder and executive director, Holy Land Trust*

"Lederach waters the dream of reconciliation in our theological garden, compelling us to transform conflict as part of the Christian mission. With decades of experiments putting hands and feet on pacifist Christian theology, Lederach gives us a pragmatic guide for loving our enemies—at home and far away."
—*Lisa Schirch, director of human security, Alliance for Peacebuilding*

"In this deeply important and beautifully written book, John Paul Lederach offers a path to peace borne out of wisdom gained from years of experience both locally and globally. For those seeking reconciliation and peace among their families, churches, communities and, yes, countries, this is a must-read!"
—*Randy Newcomb, president and CEO, Humanity United*

"With *Reconcile*, John Paul Lederach reminds Christians anew of what it means to be vulnerable and therefore practically Christian in a world full of conflict. If you believe that all Christians are foremost ambassadors of reconciliation—no matter their vocation or location—then this book will practically prepare you for the transformation that comes with a journey that is also the destination."
—*Chris Seiple, president, Institute for Global Engagement*

"*Reconcile* equips its readers to deal with conflict within a solid biblical framework and with practical tools and skills. The additional material and list of readings from other skilled leaders only makes this book even more valuable. Highly recommended for anyone interested in approaching conflict and building reconciliation from a Christian point of view."
—*Robert Schreiter, author of* The Ministry of Reconciliation: Spirituality and Strategies

"[John Paul Lederach's writing] was central to me and to many of my friends and students in the rediscovery of reconciliation as the mission of God and the calling of Christians."
—*Tom Porter, executive director of the religion and conflict transformation program, Boston University School of Theology*

reconcile

CONFLICT TRANSFORMATION
FOR ORDINARY CHRISTIANS

John Paul Lederach

FOREWORD BY BILL AND LYNNE HYBELS

Herald Press
Harrisonburg, Virginia
Kitchener, Ontario

Library of Congress Cataloging-in-Publication Data
Lederach, John Paul.
  Reconcile : conflict transformation for ordinary Christians / John Paul
Lederach.
    pages cm
    ISBN 978-0-8361-9903-1 (pbk. : alk. paper) 1. Conflict management—
Religious aspects—Christianity. 2. Reconciliation—Religious aspects—
Christianity. I. Title.
    BV4597.53.C58L46 2014
    248.8'6--dc23

                              2014011694

Reconcile: Conflict Transformation for Ordinary Christians is the revised edition of *The Journey Toward Reconciliation*, published by Herald Press in 1999.

Copyright © 2014 by Herald Press, Harrisonburg, Virginia 22802
Released simultaneously in Canada by Herald Press,
Kitchener, Ontario N2G 3R1. All rights reserved.
Library of Congress Control Number: 2014011694
International Standard Book Number: 978-0-8361-9903-1
Printed in United States of America
Cover and interior design by Merrill Miller
Cover photo: composite image by Merrill Miller using photographs from
iStockphoto/Thinkstock

A version of chapter 1 was earlier published by *Christianity Today*; portions of chapter 3 appear in the manuscript-in-progress *Compassionate Presence: Dispatches from the Burning Grounds*; and a version of the resource "Global Conflict: Understanding Terror" appeared in Donald B. Kraybill and Linda Gehman Peachey, eds., *Where Was God on September 11?* (Scottdale, PA: Herald Press, 2002). Prayers on pp. 163–66 reprinted from *Seasoned with Peace*. Contact SusanMarkLandis@gmail.com for information.

Unless otherwise indicated, Scripture quotations are from the New Revised Standard Version Bible, copyright © 1989, Division of Christian Education of the National Council of the Churches of Christ in the United States of America. Used by permission. All rights reserved.

To order or request information, please call 1-800-245-7894 in the U.S. or
1-800-631-6535 in Canada. Or visit www.heraldpress.com.

18 17 16 15 14   11 10 9 8 7 6 5 4 3 2

Wendy and I dedicate this book to our parents,

John M. and Naomi K. Lederach

and Omer and Mary Liechty,

from whom we have found

guidance, sustenance, and love

for the lifelong faith journey.

CONTENTS

Foreword

I N MY SERMON on December 8, 2013, I (Bill) claimed that there will come a day when B1 bombers will be used exclusively to drop food and emergency supplies in the aftermath of earthquakes and tsunamis; when aircraft carriers will become floating hospitals serving refugees and other vulnerable people; and when the combined military budgets of all the countries of the world will be devoted to improving life rather than multiplying death.

My paraphrased version of Isaiah's great vision of swords beaten into plowshares drew applause from my congregation. In our hearts we were celebrating together a future day when "Nation will not take up sword against nation, nor will they train for war anymore" (Isaiah 2:4). A day when war colleges will be replaced by peace colleges. A day when the greatest minds, the most creative thinkers, and the purest of heart will be working together—strategically, courageously, and persistently—to wage peace. In the greatest sermon of all time, Jesus says, "Blessed are the peacemakers" (Matthew 5:9). And we think he meant it!

But the world seems not to have caught on. According to Lederach, there have been 236 active wars in 150 countries just since World War II. And they've shattered millions of lives. I

(Lynne) recently returned from Jordan, where I sat stunned and silent as Syrian refugees told stories of inconceivable violence and death. "There are no children left in Syria," one woman said. "Even a four-year-old can describe war and brutality. That is not childhood." That war, and so many others, rage as we write.

Sadly, most American evangelicals have been quicker to vote for war than to wage peace. We say that not as accusation but as confession. For four decades God has trusted us with Christian leadership, but only in recent years have we opened our eyes, minds, and hearts to the biblical call to peacemaking and reconciliation. *God, forgive us.*

In addition to the clear biblical mandate for "learning the things that make for peace" (Luke 19:42), we have been drawn to peacemaking for very pragmatic reasons. We have seen—up close—the destructive impact of war. Along with many American churches, we have become increasingly engaged with vulnerable people throughout the world. Called to extend mercy and act justly, we have walked with indigenous local Christians as they have become the hands and feet of Christ in their communities—and we have rejoiced over what they have accomplished! But too often, we later grieved as their progress was destroyed in the path of violent conflict. From the body of a tiny child to the infrastructure of an entire country—we've seen war wipe out everything. If we care about the vulnerable people of the world, we *must* care about peace.

When we decided to study the art of peacemaking, we heard a single name recommended over and over again: John Paul Lederach. So we began reading Lederach. Continued reading Lederach. Are still reading Lederach. And say to you: read Lederach!

But beware: though this book is biblically grounded and thoroughly practical, it is not safe. It will mess with your life. Not because you'll be called to travel the world and sit with enemies like John Paul Lederach does. You may be called to do that, but that's not the scary part. What's scary is that you'll have to face your own warring heart, your own divisive attitudes and behaviors, your own unreconciled relationships. When you read Lederach's admission that he is "capable of quickly and easily creating enemies," you'll find yourself crying, "Me too, me too, me too." And trust us: it's painful to face that.

But it's pain that leads to healing and transformation. Lederach invites us to "turn our faces toward God and toward each other," and then teaches us how to do that.

This book truly has the power to change the world. Marriage breakdown? Read *Reconcile*. Extended family dispute? Read *Reconcile*. Neighborhood conflict? Read *Reconcile*. Church split? Read *Reconcile*. Countries at war? Honestly, if there were a way to lock up world leaders until they read *Reconcile*, the world would be a different place. It might even look a bit more like the kingdom of God.

Lederach has a prophetic eye, seeing unseen realities, and a prophetic voice, calling us to live a holy dream. We invite you to join us, as we join him, in learning and pursuing God's work of reconciliation.

—*Bill and Lynne Hybels, cofounders, Willow Creek Community Church*

Preface

IN THE PAST THREE DECADES, I have had the opportunity of working extensively in many different settings around our globe, much of the time in situations experiencing war and conflict. The pursuit of peace has taken me into Colombia and Central America, Somalia, Kenya, Ethiopia and parts of West Africa, the Basque Country, Northern Ireland, the Philippines, Burma, and Nepal. I am often reminded of the classic book by Chinua Achebe. Achebe chose the title *Things Fall Apart* to depict the monumental changes experienced by his native Nigeria in the early decades of this century. It feels as though all of us are living in a time when so many things are falling apart—from the breaking up of nation-states to increased levels of ethnic and religious conflict.

Each morning, I am almost fearful of reading the newspaper to find out what happened the night before. With these realities around us, it takes a blind eye or crass nerves to write about reconciliation. Maybe it takes faith and hope.

In speaking about my work in conciliation and peacebuilding, I have struggled with knowing how to convey the challenges and rewards. I also want to show the theological underpinnings that sustain involvement in such endeavors. Before I spoke at one meeting, my daughter, Angie, gave me the most solid piece of advice I had received in some time: "Daddy, just tell stories and forget the rest!"

In this book I look at the real-life challenges and understandings of reconciliation in our world today. I want to flesh that out through the experiences and words of stories. Stories are different from definitions, exegeses, or theoretical explanations. They can take on the qualities of a person, someone we interact with and learn from, someone we struggle and disagree with, and someone who affirms and challenges us. Stories engulf both our hearts and minds. We talk a lot about stories in mediation and the work of conflict transformation. We believe in the need to tell and hear stories. We work to create a space that honors the experience shared in people's stories.

STORIES ALONG THE ROAD TO RECONCILIATION

As a mediator working in extremely difficult, painful, and often violent settings, I have found that stories are like a soulmate with whom we travel. At times we bump into each other; mostly we walk side by side. I can turn to the story, even stories told over and over again, and find insight, feeling, challenge, and solace. In stories I find myself. In stories I find a connection with others.

Conflict is also like a journey. We talk about getting ourselves "in" and "out" of messes, problems, and "situations." We try to figure out "where we are" on an issue, or where somebody "is headed" with a crazy idea. Our language talks about a journey. In conflict, more than in any other human experience, we see ourselves and others in new and profound ways, and we seek to restore truth and love in ourselves. If we take care to look beyond the words and the issues, we see God.

Deep conflicts are stressful and painful. At worst, they are violent and destructive. Yet at the same time, they create some of the most intense spiritual encounters we experience. Conflict opens a path, a holy path, toward revelation and reconciliation.

This book is about my experiences and ideas in trying to walk down that holy path. These are stories from my journey toward reconciliation. I will share stories that I have heard and experienced and from which I continue to gain new insight with each retelling. The stories are a window for looking into conflict and reconciliation.

My personal story is that of a believer, a peacemaker and mediator, a sociologist, a teacher, and always a learner. Here I do not pretend to develop a well-honed sociological theory of reconciliation nor a how-to guide for handling conflicts. I am after something different. I want to explore the spiritual foundations that undergird my work as a peacebuilding professional and academic. I want to test with you how I see the challenges of my work and the faith dimensions that motivate and sustain me.

RECONCILIATION TO THE FORE

I wrote the first edition of this book more than fifteen years ago, and my primary audience was readers within my own Anabaptist community. Anabaptism, which includes Mennonite, Amish, Brethren in Christ, and Church of the Brethren faith traditions, began during the Reformation and has continued in a variety of forms to this day. Anabaptist Christians generally emphasize adult baptism, discipleship, simplicity of lifestyle, service to others, and a pacifist orientation respecting the sacredness of life as central to the gospel. While none of these values are owned by Anabaptists—and in my case they came equally influenced by teachers and mentors from the Quaker tradition—they have been cultivated in significant ways in Anabaptist faith communities. These people of faith have given me a peacemaking heritage and a compass for my journey. I am accountable to them.

Since I wrote the first edition of this book, however, the interest in peace and reconciliation as core elements of Christ's good news has spread far beyond Anabaptism. While many evangelical and mainline Protestants and Catholics have identified peacemaking as a core value of their faith for a long time, in the past several years this commitment has become even more widespread among Protestant and Catholic churches. And we must note, peacemaking commitments are increasingly explored in depth in other religious traditions beyond Christianity. There are likely numerous reasons for this, and we don't have time to explore all of them. But I am hopeful that the ideas, stories, and reflections in this revised edition of the book will resonate with a broad range of people who feel a deep yearning and sense of vocation rising from the faith-inspired journey.

A few words of thanks are in order. I'm grateful for the wisdom and words of the people who contributed resources to round out this edition of the book. Thanks also to the editorial and marketing staff at Herald Press, who saw the potential for a new edition of this book to reach a wide readership and who helped to shepherd it through to publication.

Through these stories, I hope that readers find healing and entrance into what Martin Luther King Jr. called the "beloved community" by engaging with the messy challenge of conflict transformation and peacebuilding. Through this book I hope to provide a transparency about my convictions and also to engage in a dialogue primarily within Christianity.

If we are to take up a mission of reconciliation, we must dream boldly and at the same time respond with an enthusiastic pragmatism that makes the dream a reality. We face the challenge of aligning ourselves with the central vision of God's reconciling presence and work throughout human history.

—John Paul Lederach

ONE

The Threat to My Only Child

SOMETIMES ONE EVENT can change a person's life forever. It will stand out with a vivid clarity and immediacy even though years have passed. Such is the case with a phone call I received one evening in our home in San José, Costa Rica.

When the phone rang, I was lying in bed reading a book to my daughter, Angie, who was three years old. At the other end of the line was the familiar voice of a key Miskito leader in the armed resistance who had been fighting against the Nicaraguan government. He had become my close friend in what had evolved as a fast-moving and intense 1987.

"John Paul," he said, "I have some difficult news. I have been informed by a good source that there is a plan to take your daughter. They want you out."

Even as I write these words, I can still feel the shiver, the blood draining from my face, and the pounding of my heart.

"What are you talking about?" My dry mouth struggled to stammer intelligent words.

"I cannot give you details on the phone. We can talk tomorrow. But listen, it is very serious and includes the Three-Letter Boys."

I knew he was referring to the CIA (U.S. Central Intelligence Agency). "You have to tell your wife to break all her routines. Don't let them go to school tomorrow. Don't open your doors. Watch carefully."

The words seemed unreal, like a bad dream. I knew we couldn't talk, but I could not let him go.

"Come on," I heard myself saying. "How serious is this?"

I will never forget his last words: "John Paul, now you are one of us."

I hung up the phone and went back to Angie, who seemed never to go to sleep. My mind was racing. A question kept cropping up: What in the world have I gotten us into?

I had gotten us into peacebuilding. I was part of a team of church leaders who had been working intensely to bring together leaders of the Nicaraguan government, the Sandinistas, and the Miskito leaders of the east coast resistance. The negotiations were aimed at ending the nearly eight-year war. Other mediators were located inside the country, but they had difficulty traveling because of the tense relationship between Nicaragua and the rest of the region.

During the months before this phone call, I had become a communication link, often shuttling messages between opposition leaders located in Costa Rica and Sandinista officials in Managua, Nicaragua.

By the next day, with even more frightening information, we shuttled the family out of the house and the country. In the next weeks and months, I returned to Costa Rica on my own to continue the work. Eventually negotiations were arranged and a ceasefire was put in place.

In the process, those who did not want a separate Indian negotiation increased their threats and violence. During that restless night and many times since, I have often been haunted by a nagging thought: Peace is a noble pursuit, but at what price?

SACRIFICE FOR AN ENEMY

Many children spend a portion of their time in Sunday school memorizing John 3:16. This most-popular verse has taken on a whole new meaning for me since our time in Central America and my work these past years in the context of wars. We have traditionally understood John 3:16 as a creedal formula. We tend to place the emphasis on the part that says, "Everyone who believes in him may . . . have eternal life." What counts, in terms of faith, is the belief.

Look again. Embedded in the verse is a story of a parent who gave up a child. As parents who have had our child threatened, Wendy and I experienced this story as all too real. I have never experienced anything as precious as the gifts of our firstborn, Angie, and her younger brother,

John 3:16

"For God so loved the world that he gave his only Son, so that everyone who believes in him may not perish but have eternal life."

Joshua. Even with all the challenges, the energy, the sleepless nights, and the sibling fights, nothing matches the gift of a life placed in our hands for nurture, love, and growth.

This is why the phone call shook me awake and made me see things differently. I was faced with the reality of ultimate sacrifice. When I said I could feel the blood drain from my face as I listened to the words from the phone that night, I meant it literally. I felt an immense internal sense of my heart being crushed.

I could face a threat against me, but how could I face a threat to my only child? What activity could be worth the cost of losing my daughter? Was pursuing peace in Nicaragua worth the life of my child? Think about it. Is there anything that is so important to you that you would give up your child to achieve it?

In John 3:16, we learn that this sacrificial choice is at the heart of God's search for reconciliation. As a father and a human being, I find it incomprehensible that God, as a parent, gave up this most precious gift to reconcile erring and belligerent enemies with himself.

I can understand sacrifice for family or friends. For example, I would not hesitate to give a risky blood transfusion or endanger my life if it meant saving the life of my child. However, to do this *for enemies* is beyond understanding.

I can no longer take John 3:16 as a short formula for salvation. I can only understand it as a foundational principle of reconciliation. It is an ethic based on willingness to make the ultimate sacrifice on behalf of an enemy. It is an ethic undergirded by and made possible only through the immeasurable love and grace of God.

I have experienced that love in many ways, from the protection of our family in Central America to grace that covers a multitude of shortcomings. I aspire to bring this love to the world, but I recognize that I barely understand its real height or depth. Time and again I find that I fall short. I am much less able to practice and live by it fully. I only know that this love ultimately sustains life and is the essence of God's very nature, the God who seeks reconciliation with the enemy through self-sacrifice.

PEACE: UTOPIAN FANTASY OR BIBLICAL DREAM?

Over the years I have worked—and I continue to work—in settings of protracted conflict and wars. This work has always left me with a sense of fragility, as the story behind the phone call shows. Yet there is more than the personal side. Wars emerge for such complex reasons and with so many levels of activity and consequence. These reasons arise from histories of animosity and strife between people that date back generations. They involve nations and their powerful and mixed interests.

Christians often talk of peace. Sometimes we mean the personal, interior kind of peace, in which a person feels right with God. Other times Christians use the word *peace* to talk about harmonious relationships with family members, friends, and coworkers. For many churches, that's about as far as the talk of peace goes. Discussing the type of peace that refers to right relationships on a national or global level can feel threatening, or politicized, or simply beyond our capabilities to imagine. Building international conciliation and peace is an enormously complex task, and many of us feel powerless to even pray in informed ways. We may think that we have nothing to offer; if we have trouble living peaceably with our families or our sisters and brothers in church, how can we even presume to offer anything in the face of protracted international conflicts? In the midst of war, we find it difficult to understand the feelings and perceptions of the people involved. We want to assist and help create the space for reconciliation, uprooting the ferocious weeds of war so that peace can be planted, but that goal appears remote. Most of the time it seems to be hopeless—a utopian dream.

For some time I have been interested in this human activity known as dreaming. My first encounter with dreaming at an explicit level came in the form of a question put to me: "What do you want to be when you grow up?" I found this question more annoying as I grew older. But as a child, it was exciting and filled with so many options. I faced the question with the innocence of wide eyes and unlimited ideas. Everything and anything was possible.

In my family the story is told of my first answer to that query. Apparently some well-meaning adults raised this question of future vocation and identity before a few friends and me. One friend quickly said, "A fireman." A second responded, "A doctor." And then I said, with the highest of aspirations, "I want to be a football."

The process of "growing up" and "becoming mature" shifts us out of childhood dreaming, out of innocence about the possible, and delivers us into the realities of adulthood. Growing up seems to mean "getting realistic." We are asked to become a part of the real world. But I am worried about what we lose in this process. To put it bluntly, I am worried about the extinction of a particular human species: the dreamer.

We seem to have a scarcity of dreamers these days. I often cite the words of Langston Hughes. In several of his poems, he voices a similar concern. In a poem entitled "The Dream Keeper," Hughes calls us to bring all of our dreams so that they can be protected from the "too-rough fingers of the world." In the poem "Dreams," the poet advises us to "hold fast to dreams," for without them life is "frozen" and "barren," grounded like "a broken-winged bird."

DREAMING

Dreaming has to do with the simple act of connecting the present and the future. I have noticed at least two different ways of relating the present and the future. The first we could identify as futurologists, people like palm readers and stockbrokers and early specialists like Alvin Toffler and John Naisbeth, or more recent prognosticators, such as those who predict trends in technology or politics. They tackle dreaming by reading the signs and the times and then predicting where we will be in the future. In simple words, they look at what is and suggest what will be, based on those realities. This is what we call *realism*. The other type of dreaming involves *prophetic eyes and voice*.

Realism. When we look with realism at the global realities around us, what we see is both challenging and overwhelming. On the planet Earth, we are living amid a humanity filled with need. Look for a moment through a few windows into this house we humans call home. Observe how we have chosen to organize ourselves in the real world.

The last decade of the twentieth century began with the opening of the Gulf War. In the Gulf War, the United States brought its national resources to bear in an unprecedented effort to militarily liberate a country inhabited by a few million people. Yet the United States had never channeled such effort or resources toward alleviating basic human need, at home or abroad. The billions spent in the first months of that war would have funded the annual budget of the World Food Program of the United Nations for the next two hundred years. The U.S. spent more in research and deployment of the first ten bombing sorties across Iraq than it spent as a nation in this decade to house the homeless in major cities.

At the turn of the millennium, we experienced September 11, 2001, a marker in U.S. and global history. The war on terror was declared, and it unleashed another set of armed conflicts in Iraq and Afghanistan. But these were not the only wars. Peace researchers measure conflicts by battle deaths. At least twenty-five battle-related deaths in a year and we count it an armed conflict; one thousand or more and we call it a war. In 2009 our global family had thirty-plus armed conflicts and dozens that counted as wars. Since World War II, 236 active wars in 150 locations have shattered lives. Most of these would show red hot in the Southern Hemisphere of our globe, where high levels of poverty and disease and low levels of education and life expectancy all sit, side by side, with armed conflict.

As a global family, we spend a lot of time and invest precious resources making, selling, and distributing weapons.[1] At the level of formal government expenditures, we spend $1.464 trillion dollars a year to protect ourselves from each other. We call it national defense.

As a global family we spend an extraordinary amount of money on things whose ultimate purpose has a single goal: to destroy and take life.

$1,464,000,000,000.

---

1. This paragraph, the four that follow, and the sidebar are adapted from John Paul Lederach, *The Poetic Unfolding of the Human Spirit* (Kalamazoo, MI: Fetzer Institute, 2011), 10–11. Used with permission.

Not an easy figure to comprehend. It took me several tries to get the number of zeroes correct.

Maybe comparisons help. One hundred and ninety-five countries currently compose the United Nations. If we add up the sum total of the national expenditures for the *poorest* 140 countries—more than two-thirds of the United Nations—their total combined national budgets do not reach $1.426 trillion. At the same time, in 2009 the World Bank reported that half of the world's population lives on less than $2.50 a day; 80 percent on less than $10.00 a day. In 2009 the United Nations Children's Fund (UNICEF) reported that 200 million of our children under age five have stunted growth due to a lack of food and nutrients.

Food and People Rivers

If we visualize global food supply as a river, it does not flow very evenly. There are fat Mississippi-like *food rivers* flowing into and around rich countries and the wealthy. If we had a feature that highlighted the millions who do not have enough to eat, we would see how close those who suffer malnutrition and starvation live to the food river and how often the river dried up into near-empty tributaries before reaching them. In 2009, Reuters reported that 32.2 million people in the United States—one in every ten Americans—received food stamps, struggling to put food on the table.

Then, if we imagine the population as a river—the *people river*, as it were—human mobility would quickly catch our eye. People move toward jobs and hope. They move away from suffering and violence. They head toward capital cities and globally toward the North. We could not help but notice how many of these rivers' tributaries start from the seeming unending wells of armed conflict. On World Refugee Day in 2013, the Office of the United Nations High Commissioner for Refugees (UNHCR) reported 48.7 million people were internally displaced or refugees from war. Hidden in their report and data was a small fact: 70 percent of the river-flows of refugees were mothers and children. Those who flee the violence and don't make the border, spreading and flowing as displaced rivers within their own countries, reached 26 million in the past ten years. Colombia alone has seen five million internally displaced people. More than 100 million members of our family live without homes, maybe as many as a billion without adequate housing.

That is the reality of our world today. If nothing else, these windows looking into the condition of our planet tell us that we live in a violent world. Its resources are not shared equally and are not developed to meet basic human needs. Racism and fear still run strong. Health, education, and housing sit at the bottom of national and world priorities. Human conflict is resolved by whoever carries the biggest stick. When we look realistically at our world, peace seems a utopian fantasy held by people who must be a little out of touch with reality.

We must be careful, however, with our embrace of objective knowledge and realism, for both involve a subtle premise. Realism assumes that what is now and what must be in the future are the same. Tomorrow is seen as the slave of today. Too often we find ourselves succumbing and adapting to the way things are. Too often "getting realistic" means "fitting in" and "going along." We adapt and give up our dreams to fit the way things are in the real world. Thus our desire to be realistic pulls us toward looking with objective and descriptive eyes at what is around us. It keeps our feet grounded in the practical challenges we face. But we must not permit ourselves to be defined by the realities those challenges represent. Understanding the realities in which we live must not translate into a simple acceptance that this is the way things should be.

Prophetic eyes and voice. The biblical story presents a second approach to dreaming, or connecting the present and future: with prophetic eyes and voice, living according to unseen realities. In many ways, Scripture is a big anthology of dreams and dreamers. For me, this is summed up in a single verse that describes faith, as written to the Hebrews: "Faith is the assurance of things hoped for, the conviction of things not seen" (Hebrews 11:1). As one translation puts it, "Faith makes us certain of realities we do not see" (NEB).

Apparently this author did not want people lost in the abstractness of the statement. To make the practical essence of this affirmation clear, we are given about forty more verses laying out a long list of illustrative case examples. These are people who lived according to unseen realities.

For examples, crazy Noah built a boat to prepare for a flood when it was as dry as a bone. Wandering Abraham left his home to receive his inheritance without even knowing where he was going. Spunky Sarah continued to act like she was going to have a baby even though she was far past the usual childbearing age.

These models of faith, these people, these biblical dreamers— these are known as the cloud, the "cloud of witnesses" (Hebrews 12:1). Their dreaming did not predict the future according to the present. Instead, quite the opposite is true. They changed present reality by living according to a vision of the future. We are told that this is "faith" (Hebrews 11:39). These people did not live by the way things are but according to a vision of things not seen. That vision of things not seen eventually changes the way things are.

Clarence Jordan once translated this verse as saying, "Faith is turning dreams into deeds." Proverbs tells us, "Where there is no vision, the people perish" (Proverbs 29:18 KJV). To put it bluntly, "Dream or die!" This is not a literal death, but it is a death of accepting and accommodating to the way things are instead of living as if they could be different.

We'll return to this idea of biblical dreaming at the end of the book. For now, let me just say that to take up the journey of reconciliation, we need both. We have to keep our *feet on the ground*, connected to the challenge of current realities, and we need *our head in the clouds*, with the capacity to live into a new reality of more just, equitable, and peaceful relationships.

TOWARD A SCRIPTURAL UNDERSTANDING

I am consistently faced with perplexing questions: How do we move from merely talking about peace to actually building peace? How can we promote a concern for human life and justice in settings of devastating violence and oppression? How do we bring enemies together?

I spend much of my time working with and between enemies. Frequently, in Nicaragua, Somalia, the Philippines, and Nepal, I am with people who threaten and feel threatened by others. Enemies have killed some of their friends, and they have killed their enemies. They are suspicious, and they are suspected. They have been hated, and they have hated. They place blame for suffering on their enemies, and they justify the use of violence on the basis of protecting their very survival.

As a person involved in peacebuilding, I have also become more absorbed with studying enemies. How do I work with them and between them? How can I ever accept and deal with their intense levels of fear and hatred?

From such real-life experiences and questions, I have returned to and struggled with understanding various images of enemies found in the Bible. That crazy phone call was the first time that I had come face-to-face with an enemy who truly wanted to harm me and those I loved. I have lived through various time periods of threats to my life and even survived occasions of direct physical harm. The events of that night and the years of work since have led me to reconsider two seemingly contradictory biblical images of enemies found in the Bible: the cry to crush the enemies, and the call to love them. The Bible has been a rich resource for Christian peacemaking in part because it offers both honest cries of humans for vengeance and retribution for their enemies and the persistent, gentle call of Christ, whose life and ministry provided an example of loving enemies.

The chapters that follow are not straight biblical exegesis. I am not a theologian prepared with formal tools of hermeneutics; I am a practitioner who writes from the basis of experience and builds toward understanding from that inductive basis. Sometimes I call myself a recovering academic. When I meet with people who have suffered from small- and large-scale conflict and violence, our conversations begin and end with stories. I listen to stories, and when I approach the Bible what I find are the extraordinary breadth and depth of human story interacting with divine presence. My attempt here will be set within and around stories, since I believe that God encounters us through the specific narratives of our lives and those of others. These chapters explore biblical windows on the landscape of reconciliation, and they do not move entirely chronologically. Through these windows, we can better view the heart of God and the promises of reconciliation for humanity.

As a starting point, let's turn first to the story of Jacob and Esau, two brothers born into conflict who experienced deep brokenness, years of separation, and eventual reconciliation. The dramatic story of this great biblical family offers a framework as we begin this journey toward understanding God's intention that all of us would turn our faces toward God and toward each other.

TWO

Turning toward the Face of God: *Jacob and Esau*

M ORE THAN ANY other biblical text, the story of Jacob and Esau has shaped the way I understand the journey and encounters present in reconciliation processes. This provocative story of a family and two brothers provides a guiding framework for the other stories and ideas that I explore in this book, and it offers a point of reflection for members of all the Abrahamic faiths—Christians, Jews, and Muslims—a common story of protracted conflict. Embedded in this story are many elements that parallel the difficulties we face in broken relationships. Complex and difficult encounters and brokenness occur in this story. Conflicts like these enable us to look carefully at ourselves, to turn and face those we fear or who may wish us harm, and ultimately to explore how we find the presence of God among us.

In workshops or lectures, I prefer to retell this story as a drama, of sorts, with people representing the main characters in the family. In this way we can, as the story unfolds, attend to what each person must be experiencing and thinking. We are able not only to "listen inside" but to notice the physical movement of conflict. The events of this story raise the most significant questions about the nature of reconciliation itself.

As I tell the story in these pages, I will try to lift forward this internal experience and physical movement. The biblical portrayal of these brothers poses some daunting questions that do not have answers, questions we face over and over again in our journey to respond faithfully in the midst of deep human conflict.

This great biblical family has all the challenges and difficulties of any normal family. We sometimes forget this when we read the narrative in Genesis 25–33. Let us proceed, step by step, looking carefully at the story (in alternate font) with the lens and questions of reconciliation (in regular font). Let's take time to fully acknowledge the human experience unfolding.

BORN INTO CONFLICT

Isaac and Rebekah have long awaited the miracle of a child. When finally she becomes pregnant, there is much joy, yet Rebekah feels a struggle between the two babies inside. When she inquires of the Lord, the response comes back that the second-born shall lead the first.

Let us place ourselves in the perplexing world of Rebekah. Why such a struggle? Why has one child been preferred over another? And let us not remove ourselves from the biblical tradition of questioning the Creator: Why, God? Why, after all these years of waiting faithfully, would the arrival of the gift of life come with indication of looming struggle? And before we leave this very early pre-birth moment: How do we understand and address the challenge that too many children in this world are born into social, cultural, and political structures with existing hierarchies of exclusion, struggle, and injustice? In so many places in the world, children are literally born into conflict, into divided identities, into forms of injustice beyond their control.

Esau comes out first, red and hairy. As the firstborn, he becomes the pride of his father's eyes, a hunter and strapping bulk of man. Jacob, the twin who came out from the womb clinging to his brother's heel, is the pride of his mother's eyes, staying near home and gifted in cooking extraordinary stews.

We don't have to go far to imagine the building tensions within the family, the differences between parents and children in these growing-up years. Do Isaac and Rebekah talk about their two boys? Do they talk about their differences and preferences? Does she ever tell Isaac about the voice in the night that said Jacob should be the leader? Does Isaac ever push Jacob to be like his brother? Do the brothers ever talk, alone, about their likes and dislikes, their hopes and fears? We never have the full story, do we? We can only imagine and see the division growing within the family.

In their late teens, the pattern between the twins continues. One week Esau goes far and wide on a hunt, with little luck. Famished, he arrives back to find his brother cooking one of his famous stews. Exhausted, Esau asks for a bowl. Jacob looks up and says, "If you give me your birthright, I will give you my stew." Caught off guard, Esau reacts immediately and bluntly, much like his personality. "Of what use is a birthright if I die today? Give me food. It is yours." The exchange takes place: stew for birthright, food for status and first position.

The biblical story captures Esau's thoughts that his brother's name—"the one grabbing the heel"—is right and proper in that it connotes a wily, tricky person. Inside his head and heart, what is Esau thinking? What is my brother up to? Who does he think he is? Always so superior-acting, treating me like I'm an idiot. And what is going on inside of Jacob? Clearly he knows of the birthright. Is he bitter that being a twin he is called the second one, the lesser one? Does he resent his brother's strength and close relationship with his father?

So much of conflict sits inside of us, with our perceptions and the stories that we start to tell about ourselves and others. And so much of conflict bubbles in the emotional but mostly unspoken process of interpreting the meaning of our relationships. It never is just about the facts. It is about the meaning, feeling, and interpretation of our intertwined lives. We see this here, with the two brothers. We can intuit that the story is building toward division. In their unspoken inner worlds, deep questions emerge. These omnipresent questions rise repeatedly in every conflict. Who am I? Who are you? Who are we?

PASSING THE BLESSING

When Isaac is old and nearly blind, he calls Esau. The time has come to pass the blessing to the firstborn. "Go," he says. "Find my favorite game. Prepare it well. I will eat and then give you the birthright." Esau sets out to hunt for game to roast as the meal preceding that generational blessing. While he is gone, Rebekah, with a sense that the moment had arrived for Jacob to rise to the promised right and to become the blessed one in the family, finds Jacob and shows him how to trick the old man into believing he is Esau.

They exchange an interesting conversation, for this is no casual practical joke. It is conscious, explicit deception and lying to the extent that the skin of a goat covers Jacob's arm to make him feel like his brother to their father, who has trouble seeing. When he hears the plan, Jacob is uncertain, fearing he will be caught and cursed. But Rebekah convinces him, and in a short while, he enters the tent of his dying father.

Jacob calls out, "Father, I am Esau. I have your stew. Eat. I am here for your blessing." The old man turns, uncertain of the voice, but he cannot see. "Esau, is that you? So soon?"

"Yes," Jacob lies again, invoking the very name of the divine. "The Lord your God gave me success." The old man wants to feel his hands and arms, saying, "It is the voice of Jacob but the arms of Esau." He eats and then gives Jacob the blessing of the firstborn.

Within a few minutes, Esau returns and brings the prepared meal to his father. "I am Esau," he says. "Father, here is your meat." Isaac, surprised, gasps, "Who brought me the meat? I have eaten and gave him the blessing and he will be blessed."

Isaac starts to tremble as Esau, realizing he had been tricked, cries to his father almost as if the old man had not understood. "No, Father, it is me. I am Esau, the firstborn. I am here for my blessing."

Isaac again repeats that the blessing has been given and he has no blessing for Esau. Esau bursts into a loud and bitter cry. Three times he implores his father, and on the last, with a sense of despair and deep injustice, cries, "Father, have you saved no blessing for me?" Isaac responds with words of utter finality. "I have given the blessing to your brother. I have no blessing for you. It is done." And then he adds, "You will for the rest of your life kneel at the feet of your brother."

Esau begins to weep uncontrollably. He leaves his father's tent, a bitterness growing in his gut, and shouts with a voice that carries out across the village, "The liar! He stole my birthright and now my blessing. Where is my brother? When I find him I will kill him!" Jacob, at the urging of his mother, has fled. These are the last words he hears upon leaving the village. These are the last words we hear from Esau until the brothers meet years later. The brothers are bitter enemies.

Take a minute to feel the depth of this event and to place yourself into the shoes of each member of this family.

Rebekah, with a sense that this is fulfillment of the words, must at the same time be horribly torn apart inside. She supported her son to trick her husband, and now she hears the gasp of a dying man and the bitter tears of her own son's cry that he will kill her beloved youngest. One can hardly imagine the turmoil she must experience: the guilt, the questions, the fear. We don't hear again from Rebekah. She will never see Jacob again. She will die with a broken family. I imagine that in her last days, her question over and over again is an unanswered *why*. Why me? Why us? Why, God?

Isaac is so old that he can no longer rise from his bed. He cannot see. The son whom he loved dearly has just left the tent, embittered and angry. Three times he told his son he had no blessing to give him. The other son, his own flesh and blood, had deceived him and is now fleeing the village. If the two ever meet, one can only imagine the violence that would explode. His own wife took part in the lies, though it remains unclear when and if he fully knows this. In his last days, his family has fallen into chaos and brokenness. Everything and everyone he cared about has been lost. Confused, frail, and broken. Why me? Why us? Why, God?

Esau has tears of pain and deception streaking down his face. They turn toward frustration and anger. What I have done to deserve this? He must ask that question over and over again. His mother joined his brother to deceive him and his father's last words were that he, the innocent victim of this injustice, will serve the very person who perpetuated it? His voice screams inside and out that revenge must be taken to account for this loss of honor. There is a deep irony in the biblical text. We know very little of what happens with Esau until nearly twenty-five years later. We do not hear the story of his life and experiences.

Perhaps the only person in this story who truly had a level of innocence suffered the greatest injustice. But we are not given a window into his world. We can only imagine that, on that day when everything fell apart, his questions must have been: Why me? Why, God?

Jacob is fleeing. He only had time to grab a few things, and now he is running toward an unfamiliar land, where he will be as a stranger. His heart must be pounding. His head must be overwhelmed with questions: What have I done? The confusion rattles around inside, though for the moment his only thought is to get as far away as possible from his brother. He knows the wrath and the strength of Esau. If he did not run, he would surely die. Once departed, Jacob will never again see his mother or his father. Those few minutes of deception were the last thing he will ever experience with them. Why me? Where will I go? Why, God?

THE MOVE AWAY

We find here several key elements related to reconciliation. In reference to Esau, I am struck by the power of the image of a person who was just deceived and robbed of rights having to hear the words of his own father: "You will kneel at the foot of your brother." Perhaps the most difficult aspect of reconciliation has to do with the experience of humiliation. This story will not return to follow how Esau works through the trauma, pain, and loss. I find it hard to fully fathom when I put myself in Esau's shoes.

In my experience, *humiliation*—the lived experience of disrespect and exclusion without some form of authentic acknowledgment of the harm or hurt received—leaves deep personal and social scars. Yet very little is noted in the story of Esau's personal journey through this experience. We have a sense many years later that perhaps he found his way; he comes, after all, with hundreds of horsemen riding with him. But if we are serious about the human experience of deep humiliation and harm, we will have to be engaged in finding ways to restore dignity. More often than not, this begins with acknowledgment, something that does not happen in this story. To this question of dignity and acknowledgment we can return in later chapters, particularly in the ways in which Jesus' relationships often found him reaching out to touch people, to make them visible again, to hold their humanity with care—in other words, to restore their fundamental dignity as human beings.

In reference to Jacob, we have a riveting image of conflict. Jacob has caused much of this harm. We do not know from the text if he immediately regrets this. We know that the event causes such a severe reaction that he fears for his life. He runs. He turns his face away from his brother and his family. He turns his face away from the conflict. Conflict often takes this form. We tend to move both physically and emotionally away from the source of pain and anxiety.

As a mediator, my natural tendency is to encourage people to find a way back into conversation. But this story raises a startling set of questions: Is moving away from the conflict—having space and time at a distance from the source of the pain—needed? What is required when people need distance from each other? How long does one let the distance and emotional divide fester?

We will find hints about this in the next sections of the story, but we should not minimize that moving away, seeking space apart, has a place in the choreography of reconciliation. And we must recognize that forcing someone into engagements and relationships, which we often do under the rubric of spiritual obligation, without fully attending to the preparation and authenticity of that choice, is equally damaging.

THE TURN TOWARD

The brothers live apart for a long time: nearly twenty-five years. They have no communication between them. Jacob, in the land of his uncle, finds new prosperity and marriage. He also experiences deception for the first time in his life. It requires him to work additional years to gain the hand of the woman he wishes to marry and to attend to the rising conflict with his uncle's family. The Lord speaks again in the midst of his turmoil. "Go back to the land of your father. I will be with you."

And Jacob turns and begins a journey toward the land of Seir. He turns his face toward Esau.

In these simple passages in Genesis 31 and 32 we find two remarkable elements, each leaving us with significant questions, again not fully answered. First, in this journey into reconciliation, Jacob turns. His movement is no longer moving away from Esau, his estranged brother and sworn enemy. His face now points back toward Esau, toward the face of his enemy and toward the conflict. What makes such a turn possible? I have worked for more than thirty years in situations of conflict—at times between families torn apart, at times between mortal enemies who have experienced violence. I have come to respect how this "turn" toward the other represents one of the most significant and difficult human decisions. It is not something that works well if forced or obligated. It is not something everyone will choose even if conditions have been created. Yet without the turn, the journey toward reconciliation will not unfold. Separation and distance will remain.

Second, I find remarkable these words to Jacob from the Lord: "Go. I will be with you." The Bible is filled with other instances of God's people being asked to take up a faithful journey in which they were told not just that the Lord would be present but that they should not fear. They were promised that the "way would be prepared"—in other words, that the Lord would go before the people, or that the Lord would come to their rescue. Here, in the highly charged conflict between enemy-brothers, the Lord promises to be present with Jacob. This may give us an intriguing window into a profound concept: reconciliation cannot be done by proxy but can be supported by way of witness and accompaniment.

Jacob begins his journey home. But he is afraid, for soon he will need to face his brother. He sends out some of his men to inquire about his brother, to let him know that Jacob is coming and that he hopes to find favor in the eyes of Esau. They return with bad news: Esau is coming with hundreds of men at his side. Distressed, Jacob divides his camp in two. He sends men out ahead with gifts for his brother in hopes that he may pacify Esau. Then he throws himself on the ground with fear and cries out to God: "Deliver me, please, from the hand of my brother, from the hand of Esau, for I am afraid of him; he may come and kill us all, the mothers with the children."

We cannot minimize this deep human feeling of uncertainty and fear. The pathway of this reconciliation trip for Jacob is fraught with risk. He realizes that he has no control over what may happen. He must face the brother he harmed and deceived and who swore to kill him. Notice again the movement rising from this ambiguity and fear. Jacob starts out on the trip and as he has done in the past he hopes to appease, maybe to buy his way out of his dilemmas. But he cannot. He begins to doubt the very nature of the trip he is on and begs the Lord for protection and deliverance. On this journey, a common feature of reconciliation emerges. Jacob moves forward, realizes the difficulty and his own complete vulnerability, and then seems to doubt, turn back and away—only to once again take up the journey toward his brother.

This is not an easy straight-line movement. Reconciliation will never move in a straight line from A to B. It is fraught with challenges from outside threat and inside uncertainty.

THE MEETING

The night before he will meet his brother, Jacob comes to a ford in the stream. He sends his family and all his servants and everything he has across the stream ahead of him. He remains back, alone. During the night, a man comes and wrestles with him until daybreak. When the man cannot overcome Jacob, he strikes his hip out of joint and demands to be let go. But Jacob will not release him until he has been blessed. The man says, "You have striven with God and with humans, and have prevailed." In the morning Jacob builds an altar to remember the place where "I have seen God face-to-face."

Jacob then crosses the stream, climbs the plateau, and puts his wives, children, and servants behind him. Out across the plateau he sees his brother, Esau, coming with hundreds of men. Jacob then kneels on the ground, crawling and bowing before his brother seven times. But Esau, seeing his brother, leaps from the horse and runs to lift him up. They embrace, kiss, and weep.

"Why were you sending me all these things?" Esau asks.

"I wanted to find your favor," Jacob answers.

"I have enough," Esau declares.

"No, please . . . accept my present from my hand," Jacob says, "for truly to see your face is like seeing the face of God."

The brothers stay together for a short while. Then each chooses a different valley and they depart, never to see each other again.

We can easily feel the extraordinary emotion of two estranged brothers finding each other after two decades. We find ourselves saying, "This is reconciliation! We have waited for the embrace and here it is: the true sign of reconciliation." Yes, there is truth to the embrace, the coming together with a sense of grace. But there is much left unsaid and much to be explored in these few verses that conclude Genesis 33.

The night before, with whom, exactly, does Jacob wrestle? We may say very rightly that in that long night he struggles with himself, his own past, his responsibilities, his deceptiveness. The next morning, for example, he does not walk behind his family and servants; he puts them behind him. He does not try to buy or ride equal with his brother but throws himself, prostrate, on the ground. We may rightly say that perhaps in his sleepless night, he imagines his brother—his enemy—and finds himself wrestling to the very death. For weeks he has worried about and feared his brother. All of us know how the image of the other emerges and makes a presence in our sleep. The "man" said it well when he tells Jacob that Jacob has wrestled with humans. We may rightly say, as the text unfolds, that Jacob is struggling with God. We don't always imagine ourselves in a fight with God, but here it is, again, as not particularly uncommon for the great heroes of the biblical story. They fight with God. All three of these are encounters along the journey of reconciliation: the encounter with self, with the other, and with God. We must never shortcut the depth and challenge of these encounters.

Perhaps the most riveting aspect of the story is the notion of the face of God. Jacob builds an altar to remember he saw the face of God and survived. Within a few hours, he looks into the face of his brother and enemy and finds the face of God. In the midst of deep and threatening conflict, how incredibly difficult it is for us to notice and find the face of God, not in the ones who care for us and love us but in our enemies. What makes it possible to see that of God even in an enemy?

THE EMBRACE

The embrace, of course, is the image for reconciliation that most of us hold. Yet did you notice two things missing? Neither Jacob nor Esau speaks of, asks for, or engages in the spoken language of forgiveness. Is it sufficient that Jacob shows remorse by kneeling? Is it sufficient that Esau lifts him from the ground? How does acknowledgment happen? We have not followed Esau's story, so we are left to wonder: How does a man who felt so embittered with his brother come to a place where he can embrace the very one who lied and stole everything from him? How does Esau, the victim, make this turn? Esau clearly has done well in his life, as he comes with four hundred men. What if that deception had left him destitute and excluded, which is the case in too many places in the world? And what if Jacob had not chosen to kneel, to find favor? Would Esau have reacted the same way? Why did he come with four hundred men?

Finally, about our image of reconciliation: If the embrace is offered, should Jacob and Esau not live together happily ever after? How do we explain that the two brothers choose to separate again?

RECONCILIATION AS JOURNEY

This story permits us to explore some qualities and characteristics of human conflict and the challenge of reconciliation. The story also helps us lift forward questions that, whether we like it or not, will continuously be raised in the pursuit of reconciliation. As a conclusion, let us consider a few of these qualities as a starting point for opening up the nature of reconciliation.

The primary metaphor in the story of Esau and Jacob suggests that reconciliation has qualities of setting out on a *journey*. We notice that this journey has some paradoxical features. In the first journey, the brothers separate. They move away from each other. For Jacob, the journey of separation is driven by fear and perhaps a deep inner sense of guilt that cannot be faced. For Esau, it seems driven by bitterness and hatred, rooted in a profound experience of injustice.

Ultimately, reconciliation is a journey *toward* and *through* conflict. In this instance, God does not promise to do the work for Jacob. God does not promise that he will take care of everything and level the road for Jacob. God promises to accompany him, to be present.

RECONCILIATION AS ENCOUNTER

One cannot lightly set out on the journey through conflict nor conduct it without a high cost. We see the pain and anguish in the encounters. In general, we think about reconciliation as a single encounter bound to the time and place where enemies meet face-to-face. Yet in the story of Esau and Jacob, there are at least three encounters during the journey. What happens cannot neatly be bound up in a single encounter, nor perhaps does it ever happen one time and then it is over.

We will find God present throughout the journey toward reconciliation in the depths of fear, in the hopelessness of dark nights, in the tears of reconnection. We experience dazzling insight, defining moments that show where we are going and who we are becoming in our relationships. The pathway through conflict toward reconciliation is filled with God-encounters, if we have the eyes to see, the ears to hear, and the heart to feel.

RECONCILIATION AS PLACE

This journey leads to a place. In the story of Esau and Jacob, that place involves heartfelt reunion. We sometimes think of this as the ultimate resolution, the ending place. But we need to understand that the journey has many places along the way. Each of the major encounters—with self, with the enemy, and with

God—is marked by a place. A *place* is a specific time and space where certain things come together in the journey.

In the story of Esau and Jacob, these places are marked, named, and memorialized. In these places people have met their enemies, God has met people, and individuals have encountered themselves and gained new awareness. Here again is the extraordinary layered nature of reconciliation: It is the place we are trying to reach, the journey we take to get there, and the encounters we experience along the way. Reconciliation requires noticing and naming those things around and within us.

The story of Esau and Jacob leaves us with this landscape of memorialized places, the difficult journey between them, and the sacred quality of encounter. Reconciliation is a journey, an encounter, and a place. God calls us to set out on this journey through conflict, marked by places where we see the face of God, the face of the enemy, and the face of our own selves.

THREE

The Reconciliation Arts: *Jesus*

WHEN WE APPROACH the challenge of reconciliation, we tend to ask for the steps, the model, the process, the toolkit, and the techniques. This is true whether we find ourselves personally embroiled in the conflict or providing help to others in deep conflict.

When we approach the life of Jesus, however, questions of method or technique may not be the best starting point. His ministry did not rise from recipes or in the words of the environment around him or from the law. Jesus' ministry had roots in grace expressed primarily through the *quality of presence*: the way he chose to be present, in relationship and in the company of others, even with those who wished him harm.

The journey into reconciliation requires that we attend to this question of presence. While in the following chapters we will look at Jesus' specific teaching and examples from processes taken up by the early Christian church and apostles, here we want to start with a focus that permits us to look below and beyond the content and approaches employed. This chapter invites us to explore what it means to embody the reconciling love of God found in the Word-became-flesh, the person of Jesus, in his day-to-day world. That inquiry begins with a simple affirmation: To reconcile, *we must live into compassion.*

JESUS AND THE ART OF PRESENCE

On numerous occasions, Jesus faced questions about the essence of his teachings. It intrigues me that people who directly witnessed the way he lived, engaged others, and provided a ministry needed to hear certain words to make sure that Jesus was saying things correctly. It seems driven more by their need to test than to genuinely understand. The results startled those listening. In many regards, Jesus' responses align with the nature of his presence. He used simple words with profound reach that went beyond the questions at the surface to the deeper impulses behind the questions.

One question seemed especially oriented toward trapping him into choosing dogmatic alignment, which could be used against him: "Teacher, which commandment in the law is the greatest?" (Matthew 22:36). The question itself was framed in an intriguing way, inasmuch as it sought to assure eternal life and to attend to the whole of the law and the teachings. This of course suggests enormous complexity. But the answer, what poet Oliver Wendell Holmes called "simplicity on the other side of complexity," already was known by the questioner, as it could be found in Deuteronomy. The simplicity found in Matthew and again in Luke's gospel almost literally takes the form of a haiku, though rarely written as such. Visualize them in this form—taking the second in line with what theologian Marcus Borg suggests in reference to interpreting the fullness of love: the whole-body-and-gut nature of love expressed by Jesus.[2]

---

2. Marcus Borg, *Meeting Jesus Again for the First Time: The Historical Jesus and the Heart of Contemporary Faith* (New York: HarperOne, 1995), 47.

Love and compassion hold the center. These require a fullness of commitment. They emanate from the heart and gut. They burrow and rise in the soul. They fill and focus the mind. In these few words, we find an extraordinary description of *presence*: to bring the whole of yourself into the present moment in gratitude to the Source, the Creator of life. These words, chosen by Jesus, were not original to him. He cited them from the book of Deuteronomy (Deuteronomy 6:5). These ancient words come to life only when renewed each day. To the surprise of the anxious one who posed the question with a desire to test him, Jesus added that this quality of love creates an extraordinary mystery. Love of *God-neighbor-self*, which can be called "triplets of presence," form a seamless fabric of dedicated love and hold the whole of the teaching.

From Matthew 22:37 and Luke 6:36

Love your God with all

Heart, soul and mind, and love your

Neighbor as yourself

Be compassionate

As your God the Creator

Is compassionate

To reconcile begins with a quality of presence that turns into compassion. The challenge I wish to lift forward is this: How did Jesus embody compassion?

Answering this question would require a full book, if not several. For our purposes here, let me suggest three core *reconciliation arts*: qualities that Jesus embodied as a human being.

LOVE YOUR NEIGHBOR: NOTICING HUMANITY

Jesus lived in a way that was continuously aware of the sacred around him, and he had the extraordinary capacity to see the person and greet the divine in the other. As I look more carefully at the texts describing his presence and engagement, I find a person attentive, aware, and fully living in each moment. The key to this presence was his capacity to *notice the humanity of others*, especially those most invisible and neglected in his day and time. We could mention any number of examples. There was the time, in the midst of a rushing and crushing crowd, he felt energy from a person who simply reached out to touch his garment. There was the time he saw a small man in a tree, and the way he stopped in the midst of an important meeting to take time with children.

Jesus' response, in which he suggested the fullness of the law was complete in the "triplets of presence" (God-neighbor-self), may help us understand that compassion starts with a quality of attentiveness that requires the simple act of noticing the other as a person. So simple is the idea that we far too often take it for granted. In truth, I believe this simple act forms a spiritual discipline and merits exploration.

Jesus had little regard for the formal title and position—or the lack thereof—of those he encountered. He did not focus his attention on a person's social status or visible condition, including the outward expression of their suffering (although status and condition were in many instances the motivation for their seeking Jesus). Jesus noticed people in a different way. For some, their lack of status, undeniable ethnic or religious identity, and socioeconomic conditions created untouchability and invisibility that defined social situations.

Jesus displayed an audacious inclination to ignore the parameters of these definitions. Where he placed his attention, how he noticed a person before he took any account of their social status or state of being, created a light that broke through the cloud of invisibility and the cloak of untouchability, as if these outer coverings did not exist. First and foremost, Jesus saw *common humanity*. Simply put, he noticed a fellow human being. He looked past the external markings to the inherent quality of humanity that he shared with them, a quality that held a shared divine spark. He was attentive to and noticed the sacred quality of personhood.

Compassion test. Let's return briefly to the Jacob and Esau story. Jacob, following an all-night struggle, builds an altar to remember where he saw the face of God and survived. The following day, meeting his brother-enemy, he again returned to these words: "to see your face is like seeing the face of God" (Genesis 33:10). Central in this narrative we find our compassion triplets. Did you notice? The very encounters raised in the midst of conflict and forming the very heart of reconciliation were self-neighbor-God.

Now, for the purposes of understanding the startling nature of Jesus' presence and the spiritual discipline of noticing humanity around us, let's provide a small compassion test. Think back to the last three times you were approached by a homeless person or panhandler. Can you remember their face? I say this because I have noticed my own tendencies, and, to be honest, my failing of the compassion test. When I am in a hurry, when I am engaged in an important conversation with a friend, when I am deep in thought and I "notice" a person approaching me, if I want to avoid them, *I turn my eyes away from their face.* If I look them in the face, I feel a need to slow down, stop, and engage. If I do not want to engage, I look away.

To see your face: this phrase points toward the first reconciliation art found in Jesus. He noticed and engaged the humanity of those around him. A small, final note in terms of reconciliation: when we are in conflict, we are not at our best. We have suspicions. We judge. We are not open to alternative interpretations. We do not easily offer a generous spirit. And to be very honest, it is not easy to look, and look again, toward the face of those we feel have done us or wish us harm.

Present but invisible. In 1998, I was in bad car accident near Pamplona, Spain. Our car, which was traveling about 140 kilometers (86 miles) an hour, crashed full force into the back of a stopped truck. I felt the seatbelt rip across my chest and stomach. In a matter of seconds I was overcome with excruciating pain. X-rays would later show I had fractured and split most of the ribs on both sides of my chest. I was lucky to have lived. It took a long while to get to a hospital, and on the trip there I felt myself coming in and out of consciousness. Hospital staff administered heavy doses of painkillers, for which I had no tolerance. This resulted in hours of nausea and throwing up, pushing the pain further.

Late at night, a day and half later, I lay motionless for hours. Any movement set off the pain. The university hospital provided top-notch medical care but had few nurses and aides available through the long hours of night. Around two in the morning, paralyzed and unable to lift my head, much less my body—with no call buttons available and no staff members poking their heads through the door—I lost control and messed myself beyond useful words to place on these pages. One by one, the top nurses came by but left quickly. Others came and went. I have never felt so miserably low. I had never experienced being absolutely invisible.

Then a young aide came to clean the sink near the bathroom. I had seen her once before, when she had been reprimanded for doing something wrong. It appeared that she was very much on the bottom end of whatever pecking order existed in the hospital. My voice and lungs had been so damaged that I could not yet manage to speak. From my sideways view, I could tell she smelled me, embarrassing to report. She came over and I remember her leaning close, lights mostly out in the room, and looking into my eyes. "Can I help?" she asked. I nodded. She lifted me carefully, carried me to the bathroom, and washed up what had to be the worst mess you can imagine. After bathing me with warm water and putting clean sheets on the bed, she got me back onto the bed, smiled, and left the room.

I thought then and still think now that I had witnessed an angel. I felt like a person again. Until I had experienced what it felt like to be present but totally invisible, I had not fully understood compassion. It started with the simple act of someone seeing me as a person.

Jesus embodied the art of noticing humanity. In each person he found that of God. The single most significant starting point of reconciliation is noticing our mutual humanity.

LOVE YOURSELF: SELF-REFLECTION AND SELF-CARE

Of the three, this reconciliation art may be the hardest to accept and practice. We tend to view compassion as something we project outward—that is, as a presence or gift we offer to another person or on behalf of a suffering world. This keeps compassion as an act of superiority, something the healthy offer the sick. We rarely offer the gift of compassionate presence to our own person. We don't conceive of the notion that our inner self requires patience, accompaniment, care, and reflection on the fullness of who we are—light and shadow included.

If we are honest, many of us will admit to three tendencies. First, we don't carefully attend and listen to our own inner voices. Second, we don't take time for renewal and self-care, envisioning these at best as sporadic and with a sense that they are selfish. Third, we seek external validation and acknowledgment and do not value our internal criteria and standards as equally valid.

Yet authenticity of voice and personhood suggests the inverse and even goes a step further. The capacity for self-acceptance and care, coupled with practices of self-reflection, nurture the elements necessary for compassionate presence. These have a paradoxical quality, like a sense of self-confidence without being self-centered. Or the capacity to accept one's own fears, reactions, and need for acknowledgment without those seeping inappropriately into other's lives and journeys. We find, rather consistently, that these actions of self-reflection and care were very present in the daily life of Jesus, and that he, like us, experienced the intriguing inner-outer journey as a significant and challenging aspect in the expression of his faith. Let's explore several examples with the lens of self-reflection and self-care in mind.

Taking time apart. The first and perhaps most obvious examples are the occasions when Jesus explicitly pursued time apart. These came in the form of stepping back and away from the outward ministry and into a space of reflection, silence, and walking—being alone. We may envision these as the "times in the desert." What they point to, at essence, are spaces to reconnect with the deeper inner voice, that spirit of purpose and vocation, and time to breathe, pray, and reflect.

Walking with others. A second and perhaps less obvious element is that Jesus' ministry took place walking side by side with others. As they walked, they talked, noticed, and responded to daily issues. The gospel of Mark, for example, has dozens of phrases like "along the way" or "as they went," pointing to this intriguing quality.

In modern times, we think of education as taking place inside a building and seated in a classroom. This is a modern expression of *scola*, the Greek word for a "time apart" from which our modern concept of school emerges.

When I was part of developing an emerging master's program on conflict transformation, program certification required that we address a number of challenges. One of those came from a proposed summer institute that was designed for practitioners coming from the field who would participate in intensive seminars and then complete their work in a distance-learning mode. The certifying panel raised the question of how many *seat hours* students would have in the classroom. They expressed concern that this number needed to match the minimum number of hours necessary to match a semester-long course. I had never heard the concept of seat hours before, but it struck me as an extraordinary window into modern education. Students' learning and mastery of a topic were connected to how long they were seated in a classroom. I could not help but remember my grandfather, a pastor for many years, who would occasionally comment about his vocation's tendency to pontificate from a pulpit: "The head can only absorb what the seat can endure."

Curiously, if we look back across any of the major traditions of the greatest master teachers, from the Greeks to the Buddha, from the Persian poets to Gandhi, we find rather consistently that they often taught while walking! Jesus provides a riveting example. He and his disciples did a mix of walking, noticing what was around them, engaging the problems and issues present in the lives of people, taking note of the seen and the unseen, and constant conversation. Along the way we sense Jesus himself understanding more fully his own purpose, direction, and the meaning of life. A continuous flow of spaces intentionally created conscious movement between the inner and outer worlds— of Jesus, his disciples, and those they encountered.

Asking questions. Jesus frequently asked those he most trusted to reflect with him about who he was. For the most part, I have always heard the interpretation of these instances—such as when he says in Mark 8:29, "Who do you say I am?"—as teaching devices of the master for the purpose of educating the student. Over my years as a teacher, I could not help but put on a different lens of interpretation. I think Jesus was also asking himself this question.

Authentic reflective feedback requires honest exchange. If we speak only with those who agree with us, or who give us the answer we seek rather than evoke within us a deeper reflection, we may not fully listen to our deeper inner voice or perceive the way God speaks to us. Parker Palmer noted this when he wrote that just because we say something does not suggest we know what it means.[3] Self-reflection involves doing what we ask others to do when we find ourselves in the midst of a significant conversation: "Hear me out!" As St. Benedict suggested, we must learn to "listen and attend with the ear of the heart." At the core of his ministry, Jesus had this quality. If we develop a reflective ear, the externalizing of our feelings, ideas, or perspectives includes surprising moments of listening to our own inner voice and self-understanding.

In sum, self-care and reflection must not be understood as instruments for the real work. They *are* the work of reconciliation. Fully open and centered presence emerges from daily practice of self-awareness, reflection, and care. Whether we ourselves are in relationships that have fallen apart, or whether we provide support to others in the fray of emotional division, our capacity to create safety, nurture honesty and vulnerability, and be patient enough to listen rise from the integrity of our being. This will be particularly true when we find ourselves facing misunderstanding, threat, or anger in others and ourselves. When we consider carefully the healing ministry of Jesus, we cannot help but notice that the quality of his presence had transformative impact. Simply being in his presence evoked an outpouring of internal, spiritual, and deeply humane experience.

LOVE GOD: ACCOMPANIMENT

Jesus embedded himself in the life of the community. As we noted, he pursued his teaching through an itinerant, walking ministry. We noted that the writers of the Gospels referred over and over to how discipleship emerged by walking together, alongside the master. *Alongsideness*, a word not well accepted by spellcheck, provides a third intriguing aspect of the reconciliation

3. Parker Palmer, *Let Your Life Speak: Listening for the Voice of Vocation* (San Francisco: Jossey-Bass, 1999), 6.

arts. It points fundamentally to the form by which Jesus emu-lated the love of God in the course of his daily activities.

We can open this up with a simple question: How does one love God if the greatest of all teachings and the foundational act of faith is to "love the Lord your God" (Matthew 22:37)? In Jesus we find inter-esting clues to the potential answer found in three ideas. First, through Jesus, God chose to share suffering—to come along-side the human condition. Second, Jesus chose a posture of befriending people— at times inviting them to join him and at times saying he was coming to join them. Third, Jesus chose to break bread with those who, according to the religious standards of the day, were to be kept at a distance, or those with whom there was division and conflict. Each merits a brief exploration.

Three Reconciliation Arts

1. Notice mutual humanity.
2. Nurture self-reflection.
3. Accompany through committed friendship.

Sharing suffering. In chapter 1, I referenced a new under-standing about the nature of God's love when the life of my daugh-ter came under threat. I had a hard time imagining a parent who would give up a child for the sake of reconciling not just with a friend but with an enemy. It is just downright irresponsible. But the fundamental approach found in the birth, life, and death of Jesus involves such a quality of love: to care about others to the point of letting go of that which is most precious. The gospel of John calls this the "flesh" approach—when words are too cheap to use and something beyond words must emerge. The Word becomes flesh and pitches a tent among us. This was the choice of God: to become one with us, to come alongside our lived experience, to become human, and to do so with the expressed purpose of reconciling and healing that which has been broken and shattered. In sum, Jesus provides a living example of God's compassion. God chose alongsideness, shared suffering, and the fullness of the vulnerability in the human condition.

This theme is significant in our journey into understanding reconciliation. To reconcile requires a commitment to see the face of God in the other, to feel the world from their perspective, and to place ourselves not in control of but *alongside* the human experience and condition. We saw this in Jacob's story—the call he received to turn toward all that he feared and walk back to his brother, not knowing what would happen. And the promise of God was not that all would be fine, or that all would be taken care of well ahead of his arrival. The promise was a simple "I will be *with* you." We find this to be another of the "essential" teachings from Micah. In a phrase known by most of us, the prophet asks the listener what is required of the faithful—and answers with a synthesis teaching: "Do justice, love kindness, walk humbly with your God" (Micah 6:8). And to reiterate the words in the gospel of John: "the Word became flesh and *dwelt* among us" (John 1:14 RSV). If we consider this the root art of reconciliation, then loving God, the first of the three, requires a willingness to dwell alongside human suffering, to be with others in the way God has chosen to be with us.

Befriending. Observing Jesus' actions, we find what is captured by the old English verb not much used these days: *befriending.* Examples are numerous, among them Zacchaeus the tax collector, the leper, and the woman at the well. In so many instances, Jesus' best friends, the disciples, were so unfamiliar with this way of being with the impure, the enemy, the un-Godlike, that they moved to protect Jesus from these people. They blockaded access. They were gatekeepers concerning who was important, who should be in and who should be out. They pulled back. They did not want to touch the dirt or sickness. They moved away and around enemies of the faith. They rushed past on to the important business of the day, not noticing the humanity at their side. And in each and every instance, Jesus did the opposite. He stopped. He noticed. He opened up. He reached out. He touched. He walked with those near him to their houses.

Breaking bread. He ate with them. This he did more than anything else: he kept eating with them. We find here an example of walking while doing justice and loving mercy. And it begs the question of boundaries, separation, and purity. Piety is not defined here by distance and separation. It is found in the common act of befriending the other. This rather extraordinary approach—of walking into the enemy's world and sharing a table and eating with those who are left out or considered impure—brings us full circle to a core reconciliation art: *accompaniment.* The image we have of Jesus creates a lively sense of alongsideness. In his time and place, this literally took the form of walking with those who were estranged.

Over the past years, I have experimented with my training and education work by having people go on walks together—to discuss a topic, concerns, or insights—instead of having them discuss this in a classroom or small group. I find that something qualitatively different emerges when people walk and talk. I do this with my students. Instead of office hours, I will often suggest we go on a walk together for thirty minutes. What emerges has something to do with a quality of conversation that deepens and broadens. Shoulder to shoulder means that our faces are aimed in a common direction. I feel a sense of being alongside the views and concerns of the person. When I express my concerns I feel a sense of connection and support. Walking together unleashes something in the body, the heart, and the mind. There is a wholeness, perhaps related to the challenge of loving with heart, mind, and soul.

This is the challenge of reconciliation: to come alongside our own deepest struggle to understand, to come alongside the story and struggle of another, and to come alongside the unexpected presence of God in both.

MISUSING JESUS

People often inquire how my faith informs, guides, and sustains my peacebuilding. Sometimes this comes as genuine curiosity, sometimes as a subtle form of suspicion or judgment. Sometimes people express concerns that I'm not evangelizing people through my peacebuilding work, and that I ought to be more worried about whether people are getting saved than about whether they are learning to live peacefully with one another. Sometimes they wonder whether I'm not prioritizing Jesus enough in my work, and why I don't focus on helping people to find Jesus. I can summarize this theology and concern from a single bumper sticker that you have likely seen:

Know Jesus. Know Peace.
No Jesus. No Peace.

Several assumptions follow from these sentences, ones that make me uncomfortable. This bumper sticker defines peace as an individual state and one that is somehow bestowed on Christians and is inaccessible to everyone else. It assumes that peace is only available via a personal relationship with Jesus Christ. It assumes that from conversion comes peace. This has a double meaning: it suggests that individual salvation provides the basis of peace and that any service we may provide for peace (or any other task) has the ultimate goal of bringing people to some exclusive truth.

I disagree. I am a Christian, a Mennonite Anabaptist, and a person of faith. But statements like these, that assume that peace is an individual thing that only a particular kind of individual can access, frustrate me. In this world of holy justification and dangerous devils, some people despair of faith and disparage religion. Of religion, I have more questions now than when I was younger. I guess you could say I am less certain of the certainties I had when I started into this work.

Yet paradoxically, living in the face of violence has deepened my faith, in part due to the extraordinary people I have met who found their way with courage and integrity. I don't see the fact that I have less certainty to mean I have less faith. For me, faith is not about quantity and certainty. It is about the essence. The haiku thing. Jesus called it a mustard seed. In those days, the mustard seed was considered a weed. It was tiny, yet it had capacity to grow inexplicably.

So where is Jesus? The easy answer says in his life and teachings and the grace-filled presence I experience in taking steps each and every day to follow his spectacular and ever-winding pathway. Jesus is the ultimate model of reconciliation, the one who notices and stays and befriends, the one who calls us to the holy triplet of loving God-other-self, defining the very quality of our presence with others.

God in the form of Jesus sets up his house beside us so that we see, hear, feel, touch, and interact with a person who walks and lives with us. Through Jesus, we see that God's reconciling love is made present. It takes the form of one who embodies true love and dares to live a dream that it is possible to reconcile all things.

FOUR

In the Beginning Was Conflict: *Creation*

IN THE BEGINNING God created, Genesis tells us. From a formless void, the winds of the Creator gave shape to the earth. God separated light from darkness, marking the start of time and history. God separated land from water. The dome of the sky separated upper and lower waters. Plants, animals, birds, and fish of every kind were brought forth. Then the miracle of human presence emerged; we were created in the image of God (Genesis 1:27).

Volumes have been written about this marvelous act of God. I do not propose to undertake a scholarly exegesis of Genesis 1. Yet I am always struck with the centrality of this event as related to how we understand who we are, how we live and interact, and the original intention of God in creating human history. I also believe this creation story has much to do with developing a theology of conflict. Let me make several observations about this theology embedded in Genesis 1.

We are created in the image of God. There is "that of God" in each of us. How can we begin to fathom this idea that we, fragile and finite beings, somehow are like the God of history? There are many ways to approach the "image" dilemma. It is instructive to start with the more self-evident question: What, literally, is God doing in Genesis? This is better than trying to answer the far more complex question: Who is God?

If we see what God is doing, we will have at least some idea of the nature of God in whose image we have been created. The immediate answer is quite simple: God is creating. This then begs another question: What does it take to create? I believe that the process of creation is built on several different levels of activity and meaning.

Idea. Creation starts with an idea, an image. It calls for the capacity to think, reflect, and plan. In other words, this involves projecting an idea beyond oneself.

Feeling. Creation is also connected to feeling. It is not simply an "idea" in the mind. The image we have relates to a feeling at a deeper gut level. We are "moved" to do something. We feel the idea. In other words, creation is rooted in passion and caring. I cannot help but note here that the word *compassion* rises from this "gut" feeling and image. Theologians note that, in the many instances that the term *compassion* emerges in Jesus' ministry, it is translated from the phrase that he was "moved in the gut."

Action. At another level, creation calls for action. "Let's move on that idea," we say, with some passion. For an artist, the image felt moves toward expression. Action has movement, reaching out, and expression. It purposefully carries forward activity to struggle with and realize the idea. Like the process of birth, it takes something that was envisioned but not physically seen, heard, or felt, and brings it out into the world of sight, sound, and touch. Creation is an act.

When we look at the Genesis story, we see these same basic elements. God envisions and projects, reflects and plans. God feels and cares with passion. And God moves and acts in history. We too have these basic abilities. We are endowed with the capacities of thinking, reflecting, projecting, and acting. We act in history. In fact, we create the very history that we ourselves experience as real. We are ongoing co-creators of our own history, some of it for good and some of it that creates harm for ourselves and others. Nonetheless, we are participants.

CREATION COMMITMENTS

In Genesis we find that God makes a series of creation commitments. These are specific characteristics or dynamics in the way God has envisioned and built our world. Here are three creation commitments that can inform our understanding of conflict and, ultimately, of reconciliation.

God is present within each of us. In the most significant act of creation, we were created in the image of God. In this act, we find the fundamental commitment that there will be that of God in each of us. We see this through the characteristics present within us that reflect the Creator: We are each provided with the capacity to think, reflect, feel, care, and act.

We can, in a most profound way, affirm what Jacob says in his encounter with his brother: "To see your face is like seeing the face of God" (Genesis 33:10b). Humanity and each of us as persons are given the gift of life, a gift that carries within it the presence and touch of God. There is that of God within each of us. As early Quakers taught, in peacemaking we need to speak to that of God in every person.

God values diversity. The second affirmation lies in the profound understatement that God created us "male and female." "Aha!" some will say. "Now we see the connection between Genesis 1 and conflict." There is a useful and important body of literature and research on gender differences and conflict. However, I am more interested here in the basic truth present in the creation story: that God brought forth diversity.

Differences and distinctions permeate the creation account. In the first chapter of Genesis, the phrase "of every kind" appears ten times, referring to seeds, plants, birds, fish, and animals. I am left with the overall picture of a rainforest, full of almost infinite varieties of life, or of a coral reef teeming with diverse creatures.

At another level are the careful distinctions to provide order and meaning. Light brings day and night. Earth is separated from the sky. The sky separates upper and lower waters. Water and land are moved apart. Each element is distinct from the other and yet only has identity and meaning as connected to each other in relationship.

The culmination of this process is the creation of humankind as male and female. This simple beginning becomes one of God's firm and consistent commitments. If you look around your family and blood relatives, those closest to you, you cannot find another person that is exactly like you. If you search your community and even your nation, still you will be unique.

More than seven billion people inhabit earth, and yet not one is exactly like the other. You can turn your sights back across history to the beginning of time, only to realize that there has never been one person created and living completely like another. Fraternal twins, for all their similarities, have distinctions and unique features. Identical twins are soon shaped by varied experiences. God has valued and continues to value diversity.

Creation Commitments

1. God is present within each of us.

2. God values diversity.

3. God gives us godlike freedom.

God gives us godlike freedom. The third affirmation is found in the tree of the knowledge of good and evil (Genesis 2:9, 17). This tree is often seen as the precursor to the fall and the entry of sin into the garden of Eden (Genesis 3). Humans were not satisfied with what God had given them and sought to be "like God" (Genesis 3:5). We usually jump to the consequences of

Adam and Eve's decisions. If we do so, we overlook the profound insight that God, in creating them, was committed to providing them with freedom of choice.

Perhaps more than any other characteristic, this commitment defines the very nature of God and the image in which we have been created. God is free: free to do and to choose and to act. In this sense, the tree was necessary in order to provide the choice. This is the reality of freedom. Without opportunity, without choice, without freedom, humankind loses its unique place in the creation. We are created in the image of God to the degree that God was committed to giving us a godlike freedom.

HUMANKIND: A DYNAMIC MIX

On the surface, each of these creation commitments seems self-evident and rather simple. Combined, however, they make for quite a mix. Each human was created in the image of God with the capacity to think, reflect, project, feel, and act. And yet each was created as a unique individual, and each had the freedom to choose. All of this was built into the creation before the fall.

Let us take a step back for a moment and consider the significance of this aspect of creation. With purpose and for fun, I have approached this issue in seminar formats with two illustrations, each involving a question.

First I ask the audience to compare a colony of ants and a colony of Christians like the ones at their church. I want them to identify what distinguishes humans from animals. At first, with laughter, they respond with similarities: "We work hard." "We live in communities." "We are pragmatic and want to get things done." "We all look similar."

Next come the distinctions. "We think and feel, but ants act by instinct." "We have choices and dreams." "We are quite diverse within our own species." "Each of us is a unique person with a soul and a mind and a godlikeness." We note how much more dynamic and rich our life and experience is than that of ants, because we have this godlikeness, and we are individuals with minds, hearts, and souls.

Then I add, "Oh, by the way, within their colony, ants don't fight." (A number of times I've had entomologists in the group, who have clarified the scientific facts around such a sweeping comment. With good humor, we usually agree that ants do not experience conflict like humans do.) Then as a second step, I ask them to use their imaginations. "Imagine for a moment," I say, "that you have been asked by the national government to build the perfect factory. You will be given all the natural and human resources you need. There will be no impediment to whatever you wish to try. How would you construct the perfect factory?"

The question probes the issue of our natural inclinations as we think about building the perfect world. What regularly emerges is our temptation to put robot workers in the ideal factory. The place would work mechanically and without a hitch. People would be asked to do a particular job but not to think, dream, or make many choices. All the choices are already made. People are asked to follow instructions and make the product.

How interesting and ironic that such a place is set up to eliminate diversity and choice! It also eliminates conflict. When you read major novels about the future such as George Orwell's *1984* or Aldous Huxley's *Brave New World*, you see how those who were in control of the supposedly perfect world where everything works without a hitch conceived paradise as a place where conflict did not exist. To achieve such a condition in these worlds, the controllers of the world wiped out diversity and individuality, controlled information, and restricted imagination and choice. In other words, it is the exact opposite of God's creation commitments: godlikeness in each, unique diversity for all, and freedom throughout.

On the sixth day, God looked over this creation and said, "It is very good." Quite frankly, it was a mess: a dynamic, rich, and wonderful mess. In my view, this is the central point of the creation commitments. The very elements that make human experience rich and dynamic, the characteristics missing in the experience of ants, are the elements that make conflict inevitable. By way of God-commitments in creation, conflict was, is, and will be a natural part of the human experience. By the very way we are created, conflict will be a part of the human family.

Let us push this a bit further. Most of us recognize that conflict is a part of our lives and relationships today. However, there tends to be a common and rather strong perspective within Christian circles that conflict represents the presence of sin. Recognition of our fallen nature leads to the general perspective that conflict is in fact sin. On the other hand, God's creation commitments provide a different viewpoint. Built into God's original plan before the fall, humankind was conceived in such a way that made differences and conflict normal and inevitable.

Adam and Eve were naming the animals and plants, feeding themselves, filling the earth, and being fruitful and multiplying. Can you imagine that they went about their tasks without disagreement and argument? Both were created in the image of God. Each was an individual, and each had freedom. Can you really imagine that they never argued or disagreed? How utterly boring, if that were the case!

The Genesis story sets the stage for conflict as a natural part of our relationships because of who we are, as God created us. Conflict in itself is not sin. But sin may enter into the situation, depending on how we approach conflict, how we deal with it, and especially how we treat each other. Sin is a feature of the quality of our relationships.

The signs of sin entering conflict appear when we want to be God, when we assume superiority, when we oppress, when we try to lord it over others, when we refuse to listen, when we discount and exclude others, when we hold back deep feelings, when we avoid, when we hate, and when we project blame with no self-reflection.

In sum, a Christian understanding of conflict is built on these basic creation commitments: God is present in each of us because we are created in the likeness of God. God values diversity. God is committed to giving us freedom. These elements make our lives rich, ever-renewing, and interesting. They also make conflict a natural part of our relationships.

FIVE

When Conflict Burns and We Cry for Help: *The Psalms*

F OR MANY YEARS my theology of peace, which I inherited as a child of Anabaptism and grew to claim as my own, did not push me to deal with Old Testament stories of crushing the enemy.

This finally happened when, as I describe in chapter 1, I received that horrible phone call about the threat to my child. In that moment in which I "became one of them," as my friend put it on the phone, I entered a terrible world of paranoia and fear. I connected in a personal way with the Old Testament sentiment of wanting protection and distance from—if not the outright crushing of—my enemies.

Before that phone call, I had never truly felt both threat from an enemy and hatred for that enemy. After the phone call, those emotions became real. At times my inner community of little voices cried out, "Lord, who are these people? What right do they have to do this? Who in their right mind would threaten to take a three-year-old innocent child to pursue a seemingly insignificant political objective? What kind of people would do this?"

My sense of anger and injustice only increased with the knowledge that behind the threats were nameless and faceless beings. I had become the enemy of people who could hide, manipulate, and ruin lives with one stroke. For a few dollars, they could have me killed. These were people whom I would never know. I could never hold them accountable for their actions.

For the first time, in a personal way, I experienced malevolence. Through these events, my heart bypassed my pacifist mind and connected with the voice of the psalmist crying, "Lord, deliver me and crush my enemies!"

Lord, I am distraught by the noise of the enemy,
    because of the oppression of the wicked. (Psalm 55:2-3 RSV)

Destroy their plans, O Lord,
    Confuse their tongues. (Psalm 55:9 RSV)

The wicked go astray from the womb;
    they err from their birth, speaking lies.
They have venom like the venom of a serpent. (Psalm 58:3-4)

O God, break the teeth in their mouths;
    tear out the fangs of the young lions, O Lord!
Let them vanish like water that runs away;
    like grass let them be trodden down and wither.
Let them be like the snail that dissolves into slime;
    like the untimely birth that never sees the sun.
      (Psalm 58:6-8)

The righteous will rejoice when they see vengeance done;
    they will bathe their feet in the blood of the wicked.
People will say,
    "Surely there is a reward for the righteous;

surely there is a God who judges on earth."
(Psalm 58:10-11)

While working in Central America, I had been close to the violence of war. I knew war and all that it brings. I knew families that had lost parents, children, brothers, and sisters. I had friends who lost limbs and even their lives. No matter how much I knew, it was only after the experiences of direct manipulation and violence *against me* that I began to understand the deep anger that accompanies fear. I learned the frustration of helplessness and the bitter taste of hatred. In becoming "one of them," I experienced, even if in a small dose, the deep cry for a just God and the absolute dependence on God for deliverance.

Two stories from my time of working in Central America illustrate the way that people in war zones can identify with the anger and fear of the psalmist.

THERE'S THE *GRINGO*—GET HIM!

In the months that followed that phone call, in spite of these pressures and threats, we achieved a measure of success by helping to bring leaders of the Miskito-Sandinista conflict to negotiations.

As part of the initial accords, all of the leaders agreed to go to the east coast of Nicaragua, into the home areas of the indigenous Miskito leaders. For many of the exiled leaders, this was the first time in years that they had gone back. It was the first time any of them had returned openly in the presence of former enemies.

This was a time of both expectation and vulnerability. The leaders had made some progress at the negotiating table in the formality of capital cities. However, it was difficult to carry out those agreements or even explain them in the villages where the war had raged. Our conciliation team was asked to accompany the returning Miskito leaders to meet their communities and talk about the peace process. The leaders invited us to walk with them into the heart of reconciliation and all its challenges.

It seemed like a logical proposal, but it was not an easy task. People on both sides had questions and suspicions. We did not have the protocol and formality of negotiations in Managua hotels. In the villages, it was an organic process. People stood face-to-face with the very enemies they had sought to control, enemies who in many instances had killed members of their immediate families.

We traveled long days and hours by riverways into remote areas of the country. In some villages, people came forward for the first time to speak about difficulties faced at local levels with various leaders on both sides of the conflict. In one village, people went on at some length, detailing atrocities committed by a particular local Sandinista military leader who was present at that meeting.

In such situations, in which great pain and emotion are expressed, it is difficult—if not impossible—to control what spins out of the event. That night, the Sandinista military leader and several of his men were attacked and seriously wounded. The word rapidly spread ahead of us.

By the time we reached the main city in the northeast, the Sandinista sympathizers were up in arms against what they saw as inflammatory speeches of the returning indigenous leaders. They demanded that no further speeches be made since they created conditions ripe for violence.

Puerto Cabezas was the largest of the Miskito centers. The indigenous leaders insisted on holding a public meeting to talk about the peace process, in accord with agreements reached in the capital with top-level Sandinistas. However, the local Sandinista leaders did not approve. In some instances, they orchestrated open and violent response to the returning Indians.

As the day approached for the main event, an impasse developed. Miskito leaders said they would hold the public meeting. Sandinista leaders said they could not guarantee anyone's safety if they did.

The conciliation team literally worked day and night to stave off violence, but inevitably the situation deteriorated. The open meeting was set for noon. We decided that in tune with our work, we would accompany Indian leaders throughout the day, hoping that our presence would make violence less likely.

The day before, we had separate meals with both sides and again pleaded for restraint. In the morning before we left the house, we gathered to pray as a team. In our prayers, we named leaders and key persons on all sides, those who were friends, and those who we knew were angry and volatile.

Shortly thereafter, it became clear that a worst-case scenario was developing. The meeting was to be held in the baseball stadium. During the morning people gathered in the stadium. Soon mobs began to appear, particularly groups of Sandinista youth armed with clubs, chains, and machetes. The speakers in the public meeting could barely be heard over the din of angry voices.

As one of the Moravian pastors opened with prayer, machine guns crackled behind us, mostly as a disruption, creating confusion. When the speeches finally ended, some members of our team accompanied the Indian leaders to their houses. I stayed with Carlitos, a fellow member of the conciliation team, to bring out the pickup that had been used as a podium for the speeches.

In the streets around the stadium, hand-to-hand fighting and rioting broke out. As we were about to leave the stadium, a large group of the mob rushed inside. They entered the only exit that we had for leaving the grounds. In the chaos, a young Sandinista recruit pointed at me and shouted, "There's the *gringo*. Get him! Get him!"

A mental image of that moment is frozen in my memory. I can look into that crowd and see the faces of young people, some whom I knew. There was frenzy in their faces as their eyes turned and riveted on me. *I* was the foreign enemy. *I* represented the United States, the enemy they could never touch. For years that enemy had been beyond their reach. That enemy was the cause of economic hardships and oppression and had provided weapons for their enemy. Now that enemy was within their grasp.

I represented America and all the suffering they could never escape. In their eyes I could see the years of frustration, of lost loved ones, of a pain that festers into resentment and boils up and out in an uncontrolled anger.

The rest is a blur of a few seconds. We made a leap for the truck and started the fifteen yards through the mob toward the only exit. The first thing that hit us was a logging chain, shattering the windshield and sending glass into our arms and faces. By the time we had gone a few feet, not a window was left in the truck.

I can still feel the blows of stones, a two-by-four landing on my shoulder, and the splatter of Carlitos's warm blood that hit my cheek when he was hit in the back of the head. Miraculously, he did not pass out as he drove slowly through the gauntlet of people throwing stones.

Minutes later we were in the local hospital, where we were cleaned and stitched up by a Cuban doctor. I remember sitting in that hospital waiting room, my eyes and body jerking at the sound of shouts or gunshots. My mind was racing with one thought: Just take me to a safe place. I felt a fear that crossed over into paranoia.

THE COLONEL

Less clear to me in all this business of enemies is how someone as well motivated and well intentioned as I am could be engaged in doing the very thing I argued against. In settings in which polarization has deepened, all of us tend to highlight the immoral maliciousness on "their" side. We are equally slow to notice anything but the good intentions, clear justification, and "righteousness" of our side. I lived under this illusion for quite some time—right up to the day that God gave me the shattering experience of seeing how quickly I could create my own enemy image.

Early in 1987, I was traveling in Honduras near the border with Nicaragua. The Contra war was still raging. Along this border, particularly in the outskirts of the remote village of Danli, Honduran Mennonite brothers and sisters had been displaced from their homes. This happened because Nicaraguan resistance troops occupied the region as their military base. They were opposing the Sandinista government. Some Hondurans hailed the troops as freedom fighters, and others counted them as counterrevolutionaries.

At that time, the Honduran government claimed there were no Nicaraguan fighters based in Honduras. It was a hidden war of great cost. I had traveled with Carmen and Luke Schrock-Hurst, who were working with the displaced families. These people had the pain of lost time, homes, and family members etched in their faces. They were victims in a war for freedom that was not theirs.

After that trip, I stood at the large plate-glass window and was looking out over the airport tarmac at Tegucigalpa, the capital of Honduras. I had checked in two hours early and was alone in the departure room, absorbed in my thoughts about the day's travels. It was then that I first saw the colonel.

The words of a young Honduran mother were running through my mind. Soldiers (whom the Honduran government claimed didn't exist in their country) occupied her family's house. "How do you take it?" I had asked, expecting some bitterness.

Her answer surprised me: "I feel pain for them. They are so young. They have so little hope. They know only death."

I was trying to sort through her experience, which I could barely understand, when the sirens in the airport went off. There was instant action. Soldiers hustled across the runway to a fleet of helicopters, which slowly rose and filed off toward the mountains bordering Nicaragua. From my spot at the window, I could see it all. Is this a drill or the real thing? I wondered.

The helicopters would quickly arrive at the areas I had just traveled, probably to support Contra fighters. A little less than an hour later, the helicopters started flying back. One by one they came over the crest of the hill, flying low, floating a few feet above the ground. One of the war birds peeled off and came directly toward the terminal. The wind from its rotor slammed the door shut a few feet from where I stood. The noise was deafening.

The chopper settled down a few yards from the window, so close that I could see the pilot. His face was taut, his eyes hidden behind dark Ray-Bans. The side door of the helicopter flew open, and out jumped a passenger. He wore civilian clothes and carried a small duffel bag.

The passenger ran to the terminal door, joked a bit with the customs officials, and then jumped across the customs table. Just then I sat down, and he sat beside me. He was American. He did not pay taxes or show a passport or ticket.

The Honduran pilot took the helicopter to join the fleet across the runway. About an hour later, his American passenger left on a flight to San Salvador.

My flight was late arriving from New Orleans. I waited and watched as people slowly filled up the seats around me. A truck pulled up past the window, and a Honduran military official stepped out. He was dressed in a green fatigue jumpsuit, black boots, and dark glasses. The official walked right past the window, and I recognized him as the pilot of the helicopter I had seen earlier. He was a big man, well muscled, almost exploding out of his suit.

A perfect Rambo! I thought. Who is this man? Does he really believe in what he is doing? What did he just do on the border, this very afternoon? Whose lives did he take? My mind was racing with the images I had just seen in Danli.

As he entered, customs officials smiled and called him "*mi Coronel.*" He spoke briefly with them, then went back out the door. There he stood, waiting for the flight to arrive from the United States, the same one that I would take to Costa Rica.

Within minutes that plane pulled up to the terminal. As we waited to board, the arriving passengers filed past the window on their way to the immigration and customs room. The colonel was waiting for someone on that flight.

This should be interesting, I thought. Who are you picking up this time, *mi Coronel*? What mercenary for freedom will you escort this time? A righteous disdain floated in my pacifist mind as I positioned myself to get a better look at the coming encounter. What secrets are held in your mind? Who are your contacts? Is this not the very evil of the war itself? American and Honduran militaries ganging up against oppressed Nicaraguans!

The colonel moved toward the plane to meet his friend and disappeared from my sight. A few minutes later, he reappeared. His arm was around a ten-year-old girl. Metal braces supported her thin legs. She was smiling and waving and trying to walk all at once.

The muscular body of the colonel seemed engulfed by her enthusiasm. He tried to find a way to help her. First he tried to take her hand and then awkwardly put his arm behind her to support her back.

They slowly made their way past my window. His Ray-Ban glasses were off. For a moment he looked through the window at me, and our eyes met. What I saw startled me. The colonel was a father like me! It was a metaphorical moment of stunning insight.

To this day, I carry that image of the colonel with me. I still try to understand and learn from what happened in those moments. I never spoke with the colonel. I never shook his hand. I do not know who he was or what involvement he had in the war. But I do know that in the space of a short time, I had created the image of an enemy.

Lay aside all the other factors, from social conditioning to real physical threat. In the end, an enemy is rooted and constructed in our hearts and minds and takes on social significance as others share in the construction. From my own experience, I have learned that critical steps need to be taken to construct an enemy. Each step is in the story of the colonel.

BE CAREFUL ABOUT WHAT YOU HATE

Here is another paradox of reconciliation. We must learn how to develop a positive identity of self and group that is not based on criticizing or feeling superior to another person or group.

In Christian circles we claim to hate the sin but love the sinner. I believe this is much more complex than it appears on the surface. It is filled with intricate trappings of self-deception and superiority. I have found it more honest to say to myself, "Be careful about what you hate. You may find that like a blindfold it removes your ability to see. Look first for what you see of yourself in others. Love the sinners, and see yourself in them. There you will find God."

My encounter with the colonel was an internal holy ground, a place I have marked on my journey toward reconciliation. That day outside the Tegucigalpa airport, God was in the burning bush. The encounter still has the power to shake me. It represents one of the things I find most scary about my work.

How to Create an Enemy

1. Separate yourself from the person.

First, to construct an image of the enemy, I must *separate* myself from another. In my mind and rooted in my heart, I begin to see in another person, not the sameness we share, but the differences between us that I identify as negative. I attach to those differences a negative judgment, a projection that this person is a threat to me and is wrong. Inside, hidden, unexplored, and unrecognized, is a question about myself, who I am, and what I believe. In a subtle but critical way, the enemy is connected to my own self-view and identity. Who I am is defined by who I am not. The origin of enmity lies in a self-definition built on a negative projection about another. I imagine that the other person is completely bad and that I am completely good.

2. See yourself as superior.

A second phenomenon goes hand in hand with separation. I see myself as superior. Superiority is the qualitative opposite of what we see in the example of Jesus emptying himself (Philippians 2:7). Jesus, though in the form of God, did not regard his position as superior. Instead, he humbled himself to take the form of a common person, even a slave. In other words, he sought to bring compassion by being like others. He recognized and embraced his sameness. He could see himself in the other. He chose to take his place as a servant. When I feel superior, I believe I am not only different from but better than the other person. It is the incarnation story in reverse. Though I am in the form of a common person, the same as others, I raise myself above them and take the position of God. To construct an enemy, we must both lose sight of our sameness and create a sense that we are superior.

3. Dehumanize the other person.

Third, separation and superiority lead to dehumanizing the other person(s). I dehumanize when I deprive people of the qualities that make them humans. I rob them of being created in the image of God. I lose the sight of God in their faces. I no longer see "that of God" in them. To construct an enemy, I must both dehumanize the other and "de-Godize" the other in the sense of denying God's image in that person.

What I did in a matter of minutes with the colonel carried these elements and dynamics. I separated myself from him. I saw myself as morally superior. I felt a certain righteousness about myself. I saw myself as good. I saw him as evil. My own identity as a peacemaker became more impermeable to the degree that I cast him as my opposite, a war-maker. He was less than I was. Morally, I stood above him.

What shook my very foundation was the unexpected reentry of human sameness and God. I saw myself in the colonel. I was shaken by this surprise from God: the colonel and I were so much alike.

I have lived and talked with people who have been both victims of violence and creators of violence. I have shaken the hands of convicted terrorists and people who have tortured others. I have sat with warlords who seem merciless in their pursuit of power. I have listened to freedom fighters who cry out against injustice and pick up weapons to defend their cause. What scares me the most is not how different I am, but rather how I can see and feel a bit of myself in each of them.

Every time I come away with the reminder of the colonel in my mind and with the search to find God present in everyone. It may seem easy to understand, but I find it hard to practice. Nonetheless, this is my belief: I cannot create an enemy when I look for and find that of God in another.

In the search to build peace, I set out to bring enemies together and to practice peace and reconciliation. The encounter with the colonel reminds me of a hard lesson. I am capable of quickly and easily creating enemies.

THE PSALMIST'S CRY

In less than a year, I had faced a variety of dangers. I had been accused of being a Communist Sandinista spy. My daughter's life had been threatened. I had received multiple assassination threats. I had been called a dog of the CIA. I had been stoned. The experience, now more than twenty-five years ago, has helped me understand how deeply people experience the sense of threat when they emerge from violence, whether it was in prisons in Northern Ireland, streets of Mogadishu when militias stop their car, or far remote villages with widows of war in Nepal.

No longer do I question the suspicious, paranoid attitudes of those in war. Now I know the craziness of a fearful mind that looks behind every word and thinks every person is a possible threat.

No longer do I wonder how one group could see another as a real threat to their existence. I know how it feels to be falsely accused, arrested, and interrogated.

No longer do I doubt the reality of an anger that flows into hate. I have experienced such anger from my own heart, and it is not easy to simply turn off the flow once it starts. I have been the object of such hatred, and no amount of rational argument will shift the view of a deeply held perception rooted in suffering and pain.

When I hear those powerful, almost embittered words from the psalmist, I no longer dismiss them. Instead, in so many circumstances around our globe, I am drawn to the cry that flows from the angry heart. I have come to believe much more deeply in the proper place of righteous indignation.

In too many places around our globe, I have felt and seen the rushing whitewater rapids pounding out the psalmist's cry. Reconciliation is not primarily found in the grounds of rational discourse nor in places where people have buried and no longer remember their pain. The challenge of reconciliation requires us to be present, to respect, and to acknowledge the suffering, the fear, and the bitterness as the lived experience of violence.

Reconciliation is not to quickly forgive and forget, as if it never happened or we somehow are gifted with a form of amnesia. Reconciliation requires that *we remember and change*, but with honesty about our experience and curiosity about the humanness of the other whom we fear. That is the difficult burning ground of reconciliation. I am convinced that reconciliation must touch the real experience and the depth of loss of those who have come through this difficult terrain of violence and seek deliverance and justice.

SIX

Truth, Mercy, Justice, and Peace: *Psalm 85*

M UCH OF MY WORK has concentrated on supporting local efforts for peace in war-torn countries. I find these times full of intense learning from brothers and sisters and from the experiences we shared. I may have more academic training in conflict resolution, but my colleagues in these places have waded for many years in deep waters of suffering, sharply severed relationships, and building peace in difficult circumstances.

Through the experiences, I am given many gifts: most important is a new set of lenses. For fleeting moments, I am able to see things around me in new ways. Through others' eyes I see beyond conflict resolution to reconciliation.

I see reconciliation through the way my colleagues in these places approach their lives and face challenges. They do not see their primary task to be resolving particular issues or applying a certain model of negotiation to the talks. They always envision themselves chiefly as people embedded in a set of relationships. In most instances, these are lifelong relationships between friends who had become enemies.

What they seek first is to be honest in their calling of faith and to seek what is needed in these relationships. One minute a leader can be engaged in a pastoral and supportive role and in the next minute take an exhortative and prophetic stance. They have held the hands of enemies and prayed with them. They have arranged plane flights and planned meals. These leaders of peace efforts are often more like oldest siblings taking care of family squabbles than like professional mediators negotiating a deal. Reconciliation is restoring and healing the torn-apart web of relationships.

SISTER TRUTH, BROTHER MERCY

As I traveled with members of our conciliation team in Nicaragua in the 1980s, we were asked to initiate and moderate many meetings. All the formal negotiations in Managua started with prayer and reading a biblical text. Each of the many village meetings along east-coast riverways of Nicaragua began the same way.

In most of those meetings, someone read the whole of Psalm 85. In this poetic verse, the psalmist beseeches the Lord, requesting restoration and mercy. The psalm appears in the context of a people who have been exiled and are seeking to return to their land and to the Lord's favor. It makes a plea for peace, righteousness, and well-being. In verse 10, four voices are called forth, creating a rich image.

Many times I heard this Psalm read in Spanish, with words that are different from English translations, though similar to the King James imagery. In the literal translation, which captured my attention, the psalmist says in Psalm 85:10:

Truth and Mercy have met together.
Justice and Peace have kissed.

In these two short lines are four important concepts and two powerful paradoxes. The concepts kept dancing through my mind as I watched the peace process unfold in fits and starts. For the first time, I noticed that the psalmist seems to treat the concepts as if they are alive. I could hear their voices in the war in Nicaragua. In fact, I could hear their voices in any conflict. Truth, Mercy, Justice, and Peace were no longer just ideas. They became people, and they could talk.

I started to call forth this community of four people in my training workshops on conflict resolution. First I tried a little experiment with community leaders and pastors who were working in the local peace commissions in Nicaragua. These inspirational peacemakers, at considerable risk to their own lives, were involved in local-level conciliation work, bringing together warring sides in the villages. They were unsung heroes, rebuilding their communities and starring in untold stories of peace.

In the workshop, I divided the leaders and pastors into four small groups designated respectively as Truth, Mercy, Justice, and Peace. I asked each group to treat the concept as a person and to ask one question: What is Truth (or Mercy, Justice, Peace) most concerned about in the midst of a conflict?

Each group would then choose a person from their group to play the part of their character. Then I interviewed each of the role players in front of the participants. I asked them as the characters to make first-person replies. I addressed them as "Sister Truth," or "Brother Mercy." They would respond, "I am Justice, and I am concerned that . . . " In the next step, we opened a discussion and held a little mediation session between the four people.

Over the years I have repeated the exercise with many different people and contexts. It varies each time. Unique and amazingly various insights emerge from people's experiences and concerns. As a way to understand this more fully, I have written a story that can be adapted as a play or a liturgy.[4]

THE MEETING

Greatly distressed in the midst of a nasty conflict, I kept hearing voices appealing to Truth, Mercy, Justice, and Peace. The arguments and blows had gone round and round. So finally I made a proposal. "What if," I asked the people in this awful fight, "what if we invited our four friends to join us and asked them to openly discuss their views about conflict?"

Locked in their righteous stances, the people looked at me, stunned with such an absurd idea. But I pressed ahead without paying much attention. "I have seen them come and go in other fights. I could ask them to try to clear up a few things."

Nobody objected, so I brought Truth, Mercy, Justice, and Peace into our room and sat them down in front of the belligerent crowd. I addressed the four. "We want to know what concerns you each have in the midst of conflict. May we hear your views?"

Truth stood and spoke first. "I am Truth," she said. "I am like light that is cast so all may see. In times of conflict, I want to bring forward what really happened, putting it out in the open. Not the watered-down version. Not a partial recounting. My handmaidens are transparency, honesty, and clarity. I am set apart from my three colleagues here," Truth gestured toward Mercy, Justice, and Peace, "because they need me first and foremost. Without me, they cannot go forward. When I am found, I set people free."

"Sister Truth," I interjected hesitantly, not wanting to question her integrity, "you know I have been around a lot of conflict. There's one thing I'm always curious about. When I talk to one side, like these people over here, they say that you are with them.

---

4. A version of this story, which can be used as a short drama, is available on pp. 167–72.

When I talk to the others, like our friends over there, they claim you are on *their* side. Yet in the middle of all this pain, you seem to come and go. Is there only one Truth?"

"There is only one Truth, but I can be experienced in many different ways. I reside within each person, yet nobody owns me."

"If discovering you is so crucial," I asked Sister Truth, "why are you so hard to find?"

She thought for a while before replying. "I can only appear where the search is genuine and authentic. I come forward only when each person shares with others what they know of me, and when each one respects the others' voices. Where I am strutted before others, like a hand puppet on a child's stage, I am abused and shattered, and I disappear."

"Of these three friends," I pointed to the three colleagues seated around her, "whom do you fear the most?"

Without hesitation she pointed to Mercy. "I fear him," she said quietly. "In his haste to heal, he covers my light and clouds my clarity. He forgets that Forgiveness is *our* child, not his alone."

Next I turned to Mercy. "I am sure you have things to say. What concerns you?"

Mercy rose slowly and said, "I am Mercy." He seemed to begin with a plea, as though he knew that he, among them all, was under tight scrutiny. "I am the new beginning. I am concerned with people and their relationships. Acceptance, compassion, and support stand with me. I know the frailty of the human condition. Who among them is perfect?"

He turned to Truth and continued, with his eyes on her. "She knows that her light can bring clarity, but too often it blinds and burns. What freedom is there without life and relationship? Forgiveness is indeed our child, but not when people are arrogantly clubbed into humiliation and agony with their imperfections and weaknesses. Our child Forgiveness was birthed to provide healing."

I could not resist posing an urgent question: "But, Brother Mercy, in your rush to accept, support, and move ahead, do you not abort the child?"

He reacted quickly: "I do not cover Truth's light. You must understand. I am Mercy. I am built of steadfast love that supports life itself. It is my purpose in life to bring forward the eternal grace of new beginnings."

"And whom do you fear the most?" I asked.

Mercy turned, faced Justice, and spoke clearly: "My Brother Justice, in his haste to change and make things right, forgets that his roots lie in real people and relationships."

"So, Brother Justice," I said, "what do you have to say?"

"I am Justice," he responded as he rose to his feet. His strong voice was accompanied by a deep smile. "Mercy is correct. I am concerned about making things right. I consider myself a person who looks beneath the surface and behind the issues about which people seem to fight. The roots of most conflicts are tangled in inequality, greed, and wrongdoing.

"I stand with Truth, who sheds her light to expose the paths of wrongdoing. My task is to make sure that something is done to repair the damage wreaked, especially on the victims and the downtrodden. We must restore the relationship, but never while failing to acknowledge and rectify what broke the relationship in the first place."

A question chewed at my mind, and I had to ask it: "But, Brother Justice, everybody in this room feels they have been wronged. Most are willing to justify their actions, even violent deeds, as doing your bidding. Is this not true?"

"It is indeed," Justice responded. "Most do not understand." He paused as he thought for a minute.

"You see, I am most concerned about accountability. Often we think that anything and everything is acceptable. True and committed relationships have honest accounting and steadfast love. Love without accountability is nothing but words. Love with accountability is changed behavior and action. This is the real meaning of restoration. My purpose is to bring action and accountability to the words."

"Then whom do you fear?" I inquired.

"My children," he chuckled, remembering years of experience. "I fear that my children, Mercy and Peace, see themselves as parents." His voice carried a hint of gentle provocation. "Yet they are actually the fruit of my labor."

Peace burst into a glowing smile. Before I could speak, she stepped forward. "I am Peace, and I agree with all three," she began. "I am the child to whom they give birth, the mother who labors to give them life, and the spouse who accompanies them on the way. I hold the community together, with the encouragement of security, respect, and well-being."

Truth and Justice began to protest. "That is precisely the problem," said Truth in a frustrated voice. "You see yourself as greater and bigger than the rest of us."

"Arrogance!" Justice pointed his finger toward Peace. "You do not place yourself where you belong. You follow us. You do not precede us."

"That is true, Brother Justice and Sister Truth," Peace responded. "I am more fully expressed through and after you both. But it is also true that without me, there is no space cleared for Truth to be heard."

Peace turned toward Justice. "And without me, there is no way to break out of the vicious cycle of accusation, bitterness, and bloodshed. You yourself, Justice, cannot be fully embodied without my presence. I am before and after. There is no other way to reach me. I myself am the way."

Silence fell for a moment.

"And whom do you fear?" I asked.

"Not whom, but what and when," Peace replied. "I fear manipulation. I fear the manipulation of people using Sister Truth for their own purposes. Some ignore her, some use her as a whip, some claim to own her. I fear times when Brother Justice is sacrificed for the sake of Brother Mercy. I fear the blind manipulation when some will sacrifice life itself in trying to reach the ideal of Brother Justice. When such trickery takes place, I am violated and left as an empty shell."

I focused my attention on all four. "How would it be possible for you four to meet? What would you need from each other?"

Truth looked first at Mercy. "You must slow down, Brother Mercy. Give me a chance to emerge. Our child cannot be born without the slow development in the womb of the mother."

Mercy nodded. "Shine bright, dear Sister Truth. But please take care not to blind and burn. Remember that each person is a child of God. Each is weak and needs support to grow."

Justice was eager to speak. "I have been partly reassured by the words of Sister Peace. I need a clear statement that she gives a place for accountability and action. Remember when Micah spoke of us: 'Love Mercy and do Justice.' You, Sister Peace, must allow room for me to come forward. If not, you will be aborted."

Peace responded on the heels of his last words. "Brother Justice, our lips will meet if we recognize that we need one another. Do not let your heart of compassion fall into bitterness that rages without purpose. I will provide the soil for you to work and bear fruit."

The four were huddled in a small circle. "And what," I asked, "is this place called where you stand together?"

"This place," they responded in unison, "is *reconciliation*."

Then suddenly and without signal, they touched hands and danced. It was as if the dance came only rarely, like the weaving of lines and bodies around a Maypole. I could hardly distinguish one from the other as they swung from the room. No one said a word. No music was in the air, only the images of the interwoven bodies of Truth, Mercy, Justice, and Peace.

SPACE FOR ALL TO SPEAK

I learned important insights about reconciliation from the Nicaraguan experience and from years of reflection and experimentation with Psalm 85. As suggested in the story of Jacob and Esau, Psalm 85 reinforces the understanding that reconciliation is a journey we must take, a place we are trying to reach, and encounters along the way.

The psalmist provides new and deeper insight into the idea that reconciliation is a *locus*, a meeting place. With these stories, we are exploring reconciliation as a place where we encounter ourselves, others, and God. Psalm 85 presents reconciliation as a dynamic social space where different but interdependent social energies and concerns are brought together and given voices.

Reconciliation requires us to take up the primary practical task of creating the *dynamic social space* where Truth, Mercy, Justice, and Peace can genuinely meet and wrestle things out, much like Jacob in the long night. We experiment with various procedures and mechanisms that serve this goal.

Too often in the midst of conflict, we take these social energies—we can see them as four siblings—as contradictory forces, voiced by different persons within the conflict. They are seen as pitted against each other. Those who cry out for Truth and Justice are taken as adversaries of those who plead for Mercy and Peace, and they often understand themselves that same way.

The vision of the psalmist is different. Reconciliation is possible only as each sees the place and need for the other. This approach means that each voice, and the social energy it produces, is incomplete without the other.

What does this mean at a practical level? We must pay attention and give space to the different energies represented by the voices of Truth, Mercy, Justice, and Peace. When these voices are heard as contradictory forces, we find ourselves mired in erupting conflict and paralyzed by it. We argue endlessly over which is more important, justified, or proper.

When we hear these four voices as contradictory, we are forced into a false position of choosing one or the other. It is as if they were in a boxing match that only leaves winners and losers. Such tunnel vision should not exist. We are not asked to choose between rain or sunshine. Each is different, but both are needed for sustaining life and growth. Such is the case with Truth and Mercy, Justice and Peace.

Psalm 85 shows that conflict has revelatory and reconciling potential when the four different energies are embraced. We need to recognize all their concerns as proper, provide them with voices, respond to their fears and needs, and place them in an open and dialogical setting. That is better than roping them into a boxing match, as adversaries. By letting all of them speak, they are less likely to be driven underground or to extremes. As we deal with conflict this way, God reveals the road to reconciliation.

Let us create the social space that brings Truth, Mercy, Justice, and Peace together within a conflicted group or setting. Then energies are crystallized that create deeper understanding and unexpected new paths, leading toward restoration and reconciliation.

SEVEN

Where Two or Three Meet: *Matthew 18*

I N T H E S U N D AY and Wednesday evening services of my childhood as a preacher's kid in Oregon, I first heard, enough times to memorize it, the well-known verse from Matthew 18:20: "For where two or three are gathered in my name, I am there among them." Years later, I again heard these verses used on "the mission field," by small, fledgling congregations in different parts of the globe. I think it is the most-quoted verse from Matthew 18.

Matthew 18:15-20:

New Revised Standard Version

If another member of the church sins against you, go and point out the fault when the two of you are alone. If the member listens to you, you have regained that one. But if you are not listened to, take one or two others along with you, so that every word may be confirmed by the evidence of two or three witnesses. If the member refuses to listen to them, tell it to the church; and if the offender refuses to listen even to the church, let such a one be to you as a Gentile and a tax collector. Truly I tell you, whatever you bind on earth will be bound in heaven, and whatever you loose on earth will be loosed in heaven. Again, truly I tell you, if two of you agree on earth about anything you ask, it will be done for you by my Father in heaven. For where two or three are gathered in my name, I am there among them.

It is used in a fairly consistent way across cultural and geographic contexts, to encourage a small gathering for worship. They take it to mean, "Hey, it doesn't matter if only a few of us have shown up. Take courage. God is among us."

It is true that we do not need large numbers of people for God to be present. God is present with me even when I am completely alone. But what is the meaning of these verses in the context of Matthew 18? When this verse is understood in the flow of the whole passage, its meaning is quite different from its typical use for encouragement because few people are present. The context is conflict.

Matthew 18 is a chapter about conflicts. Consider for a moment the stories and teachings. The chapter begins with the disciples asking the question, "Who is the greatest in the kingdom of heaven?" (Matthew 18:1). They are primarily concerned with status and power. Who will stand higher than another? Who will be seen as more important? Think for a minute about your own experiences with organizations, church structures, governments, and the like. Conflicts over power and status occur all the time.

At the end of the chapter, Jesus relates the parable of the unforgiving servant. Here is a man who owes a large sum of money to the king. The debtor begs for mercy and patience. The king, we are told, has pity and has forgiven him his entire debt. Minutes later, this same man bumps into a neighbor who owes him a small sum of money. He leaps at his throat and demands to be paid right away. His friend begs for mercy, but to no avail. The king, upon hearing this, throws the man in prison for his lack of mercy.

The conflict is over money and payment schedules. Does this sound much like conflicts in the church over money, debts, and payment schedules? Matthew 18 starts with power and ends with money. The entire chapter deals with mundane, human, relational dynamics that lie at the root of most conflicts.

PRACTICAL GUIDELINES

These interesting verses give direct and practical teaching from Jesus. They provide specific guidelines for how we are to proceed when we feel we have been wronged or when we feel that a sister or brother has erred.

As I ponder these verses, I have certain limitations and advantages that a theologian does not have. By training, I am a sociologist. So I put on lenses that look for the structure and dynamics of social process and the spiritual dimension that underpins these processes. I do not, however, have the tools of rigorous biblical interpretation; please bear that in mind as I outline my observations.

I take the statement "If another member of the church sins" in a broad sense (any sinning) rather than a narrow sense (only if sinning against you). This is justified because "against you" (18:15) is not in the oldest Greek texts, biblical students tell me. Peter is the one who seems to be chiefly concerned about someone who sins "against me" (18:21). But I think Jesus had a broad concern for gently restoring any transgressing member (as in Matthew 7:5; Luke 17:3; cf. Galatians 6:1; Leviticus 19:17; Ezekiel 3:16-21).

In most conflicts and especially in those involving church members, almost everybody on all sides of the problem feels that they have been sinned against. I have found this to be true, especially if the conflict has gained any momentum or has escalated.

Here in Matthew 18, a church member wants to bring correction to another member regarded to have done something wrong. I understand "sins (against)" to imply that we have a conflict in the making. I want to look into these verses for what light they shed on how we understand and respond to conflict.

As a sociologist who works from a faith basis, I have several questions. Exactly how do these steps guide us in thinking about and approaching conflict? What assumptions underlie the steps?

What goals are to be achieved? What dynamics do they clarify about relationships and handling confrontation?

What skills does Jesus assume we need? What challenges does this approach pose for us? Is this model good for all situations and cultures? How does our actual behavior look alongside the suggested guidelines? What, in the end, is the window of wisdom and light that this instruction opens on conflict? Let me start by making four basic observations.

First, in the context of the chapter and this particular teaching, the primary and ultimate goal of this teaching is to work for reconciliation. We are called to work for the restoration and healing of people and their relationships.

Second, in my opinion, these are some of the most specific and practical guidelines appearing in all the teachings of Jesus. He is not talking in parables or providing broad principles. He has identified four specific steps in a detailed order.

Matthew 18:15-20:

Normal Practice Version

When you have a problem with somebody in the church, check it out first to make sure you are not alone in this problem. There is a good chance that if you have had a problem with this person, somebody else has as well. Go and pick a good friend who is likely to understand and agree with you. If she agrees with you that this person is a real turkey, then talk to some more people to see if there is broader consensus. If money, land, or inheritance is involved, tell it to a lawyer, as lawyers were given by God to keep the church honest. If a friend, a small group, and a lawyer agree, then tell it to the church, preferably in private to the pastor and elders. When you tell them, say it is a concern that you have prayed about for some time and that there is a group of people who share the concern. Do not tell it openly in a congregational meeting since that is volatile and could get messy. Truly I say to you, from that point on, it is the responsibility of the pastor and elders to take care of the problem. Your task is to make sure they do it right.

Third, this is one of the few times that Jesus mentions, in a specific way, the church or the organized community. As such, this text outlines specific steps for how people in the redeemed, peaceful community should handle differences, confrontation, and conflict.

Fourth, while Jesus' instruction here is eminently practical, it is rarely practiced. Indeed, it is one of the least-practiced teachings in the New Testament. Let me illustrate this latter point by providing you with Matthew 18:15-20 in the NPV: that is, the Normal Practice Version (see page 96).

The contrast between the New Revised Standard Version and the Normal Practice Version shows many ways we tend to avoid and actually extend the conflict within the community. We avoid the specific procedures in Jesus' original teaching that lead to engagement, a turning toward conflict and the other. Let us look at each step and its implications in more detail.

STEP 1: GO DIRECTLY

This seems to be a logical and straightforward idea. Yet talking with the person about the problem represents one of the more difficult practical interactions in human relationships. In common practice, complainers take the problem outside the relationship and "triangle" other people into the situation. While it seems simple to go directly and talk with the brother or sister, that is actually based on a number of important prerequisites and assumptions. To understand those requires scrutiny from social, psychological, and spiritual dimensions.

From the social and psychological viewpoint, to engage someone in direct conversation about a problem I have with him or her requires a double movement. First, I must begin an internal process of awareness, dealing with my own feelings, anxieties, and perceptions. Second, I must also turn myself toward an engagement with that other person. This is part of the dynamic, eternal, and intriguing nature of conflict: It always poses a journey, an encounter with self and with others.

In conflict, we bump up against ourselves and we bump up against others. This is precisely what makes going directly such a complex process. Some of the key steps include the following.

First, going directly involves implicit—if not explicit—self-reflection. Our self-esteem always comes under question. From such a self-encounter, we become aware, an awareness often tainted by our experiences, perceptions, and feelings. Nonetheless, we are aware. In the self-encounter, we make choices about how to respond and engage the opportunity for reflection provided by conflict.

For example, if we are defensive, that usually means we feel insecure. We react to the information coming in and the anxiety it produces. Blaming is often a mechanism for avoiding the anxiety and projecting it onto someone else. If we are to go directly in a constructive way, we need to recognize the task this involves. We must face new information and perceptions and grapple with the source of our anxieties and fears. We must move toward our fears and embrace them in an explicit manner.

Second, in going directly, we choose to move toward other people. That often means moving toward the very source of our fears. This is complicated, because we will have to do two things at the same time: define ourselves and interact with others. Both pose major challenges and potential pitfalls.

Questions We Ask Ourselves

In conflict, whether we are aware of it or not, we are constantly assessing two sets of questions about who we perceive to be our "opponents":

1. What are they up to? Why are they doing that? What do they need and want? Are they right? Are they good people? How do they really see and feel about me?

2. How does it affect me? Who am I? Am I right? Am I a good person? What do I need? What am I up to? How do I see and feel about them?

It may be easier for us to move toward others with an attitude of defensiveness, accusation, and blame. Sometimes we may use the more passive mechanisms of hinting at wrongs but not clarifying the concerns. We may react to their response, counter with better and more rational arguments, and seek to win and show we are right. Or we may retreat and claim it is impossible to deal with that other party.

On the other hand, suppose we wish to go directly in a constructive manner. Then we must both define ourselves in a clear, proactive manner and create the space for interaction with the perceptions and concerns of the other party. A proactive self-definition in times of conflict is neither blaming nor retreating. It involves a stance of vulnerable transparency, where I speak from a depth of awareness about my own concerns, fears, hopes, and needs.

As a wise grandmother once told me in Costa Rica, it is the gift of "going to my enemy with my heart in my hand." Creating a space for interaction is not based on seeking to establish who is right or wrong, or on agreeing and disagreeing. It is basically a stance of connecting with and embracing their experience. It is the gift of recognition and acknowledgment.

I have identified these as social-psychological elements. Each also has deep spiritual dimensions. These are perhaps best understood as "disciplines of the soul," to use current terminology. Such disciplines are internal, God-inspired, and God-supported work, necessary for moving toward reconciliation.

I believe that this first step proposed by Jesus—this practice of "going directly"—is central for an understanding of reconciliation. It poses a series of important dual tasks. We must encounter both ourselves and others. We must recognize our fears and yet not be bound by them. We must define ourselves and also acknowledge the experience of others.

Each of these presupposes a significant spiritual dimension of prayerful vulnerability, responsible discernment, and interactive engagement. The required action is summed up in two words: "go directly." Doing that depends on a deeply spiritual and disciplined process.

Spiritual Disciplines for Reconciliation

Spiritual disciplines that enable us to enact this first step from Matthew 18 include the following.

1. Prayerful vulnerability means that we dare to look within ourselves, at the sources of our fears and anxieties. We seek understanding that emerges from beyond normal human capacities and responses. Such a discipline can only develop if we understand that conflict provides an opportunity for reflection and growth, even when we feel under siege and threatened.

Prayerful vulnerability creates a quality of awareness based on openness to others and God. In that awareness, I can learn about myself rather than defending myself. Instead of seeing myself as superior to the other person, I see myself reflected in the other, and I find God in both.

In this way, prayerful vulnerability captures the most proactive elements of Mennonite nonresistance. It is connected to the basic notion of emptying oneself, as Jesus did (Philippians 2:6-7). The Mennonite tradition has defined nonresistance as "not resisting." People tend to take such nonresistance as a negative way and to practice passive avoidance and retreat.

In contrast, prayerful vulnerability as nonresistance implies an *active* spiritual discipline. It means a willingness to empty oneself, thus creating an awareness about oneself that allows space for God. This leads to internal clarity, openness, honesty, and transparency. These are necessary ingredients for proactive engagement with others, particularly those whom you perceive as threatening. As a discipline of the soul, prayerful vulnerability is a stance of listening and learning.

2. Responsible discernment happens when we take it upon ourselves to move toward the conflict and others. The nature of this discipline involves the difficult task of identifying clearly when and where we are relationally dealing with a problem. First, if an individual member is to recognize a problem as "sin," we as a church have to prepare for this by working together at discerning what sin is (Matthew 18:18). Second, at times we fail on the side of letting things go on, expecting others to do this task or not caring about others enough. At other times, we are overly responsible and try to carry everyone's problems on our own shoulders.

Discernment is not simply a thinking process. It is primarily action with others. Disciplined responsibility involves discernment of our accountability and interdependence. Responsible discernment clearly underpins the four steps suggested in Matthew 18.

3. Interactive engagement is a discipline characterized by both transparency of self and acknowledgment of others. It is not characterized by blaming or retreating. Interactive engagement is a proactive meeting, and readiness for that meeting emerges from within. It permits persons to share their deepest understandings and also interact with those coming from other viewpoints.

Family system theorists counsel us to be a "nonanxious presence," engaged with others without worry or fear. John describes this as "perfect love" that can cast out all fear (1 John 4:18). Interactive engagement happens during conflict when we have the spiritual discipline needed for sharing transparently and interacting constructively with differences that emerge.

STEP 2: TAKE ALONG ONE OR TWO WITNESSES

Suppose the erring member does not listen to the counsel of one person and peace is not restored. Then, Jesus says, the second major step is to involve a broader group of people. These are additional "witnesses," who confirm the evidence. Having two or three means creating a body of people who begin working together to discern what is happening and what needs to be done (see 1 Timothy 5:19; Deuteronomy 19:15).

Several points stand out as we look further into this dynamic. The idea of witness carries an image of someone who is present with the people and experiencing the difficulty. In handling conflict and seeking reconciliation, presence involves a twofold stance.

First, the previous discussion asserts that primary responsibility lies with those experiencing the conflict. In other words, witnesses help to create the forum where reflection, listening, and understanding can emerge. This is different from assessing fault or judging. It points toward capacities for creating a setting where people can be transparent, engage each other, and seek God. By its very nature, such a place can be seen as holy ground. Witnesses need the spiritual disciplines identified earlier and the specific skills related to creating such a space.

A look back across church history raises an interesting question for us. Have we envisioned and developed the capacities, gifts, and skills necessary for creating such a space and presence? We have generally interpreted this text simply from the operational standpoint of assessing blame and wrong. We have often failed to exercise prayerful vulnerability, responsible discernment, and interactive engagement.

As a result, our outcomes have commonly brought retributive punishment, separation, and distance. We have often based ourselves on "righteousness" in the sense of being "right," not necessarily on holiness, which creates the space for God's presence within each person and between people.

Second, presence gives birth to accountability that can only be understood in community. Having witnesses ties the process to broader discernment. Listening and accountability belong to this approach. Accountability is a complicated idea and process. For some, it signals oppression and narrowness, having others tell you what to do, and then always having to be responsible to them. For others, it carries a more positive value. When performed with commitment and mutual submission, accountability brings freedom. We have others to rely on and help us.

At times I have felt both the narrow and the freeing sides of accountability. Yet neither captures the deeper sense of what is happening in this second step. Let me suggest a third option. The phrase "where two or three are gathered" (Matthew 18:20) refers to accountability as the engagement of Truth that fosters growth in individuals, in their relationship, and in their understanding of God.

When I talk about presence as giving birth to accountability, I do not mean whipping someone back into line or holding fast to dogmatic principles. I refer to a process that creates a space where it is possible to engage Truth. This leads us to live by the understanding that emerges from the encounter. Such a process of accountability can ultimately only be understood in community, and it necessarily draws participation from each person involved.

"Two or three gathered," as a step (Matthew 18:18-20), thus has practical and deep spiritual aspects. On the practical side, this step concerns the development of capacities and skills that help to create a safe space for people to be transparent and interact with each other. The spiritual dimension means that this kind of space is holy ground. It represents the place where we encounter God and each other. This carries us beyond "reaching an agreement and resolving issues." It leads us to deeper understanding and growth as individuals and communities.

STEP 3: TELL IT TO THE CHURCH

If the first two steps have not led to a successful conclusion, the third major step in the process is to take the situation to a broader forum, here represented by the word *church*. Take it to the believing community. In the earlier steps, I started by reflecting on social significance before considering spiritual underpinnings. For this step, let me reverse the order, beginning with three basic observations:

First, conflict and church doctrine are connected. How we organize ourselves as churches will affect how we deal with conflict. And how we deal with conflict is reflected in our structures.

In the next chapter, I will explore this more when we consider the Jerusalem forum.

Second, working on conflict is spiritual work. This has been discussed earlier in different ways, but here it is seen again. To take the problem to the church assumes a view of the church as a place to process and work with conflict, not a place that is free from conflict.

Third, this simple instruction, "Tell it to the church," (Matthew 18:17) offers a model to follow. Reconciliation is the mission of the church. Working on conflict is spiritual. It involves an encounter with ourselves, others, and God. Thus we begin to understand that reconciliation is about the transformation of people and their relationships. It means change, moving from isolation, distance, pain, and fear toward restoration, understanding, and growth. As shown often in the Bible story, the basic purpose of God acting in history is reconciliation. All things are being brought together (Colossians 1:20).

At a practical level we can ask ourselves the same questions we did with reference to step 2 (taking witnesses along). How do we make the church community a place where this mission of encounter, growth, and reconciliation can take place?

Let me reinforce the basic ideas stated in the first two steps. At the practical level, the constructive engagement of conflict at group levels requires the same disciplines that underpin the interpersonal or small-group level. We need self-definition, transparency, and interactive engagement.

What changes in step 3 is the number of people involved. This calls for innovation and creativity in seeking mechanisms for expressing conflict in larger groups, ways that are both responsible and constructive for the people involved. The keys lie in two elements: We need to understand that working with and through conflict is normal, spiritual work. We also need to develop the disciplines and skills to do that work with larger groups of people.

Next we return to our idea of responsible discernment. One of the most difficult tasks facing church leaders is to discern the nature of the conflict. Then they can develop a forum or process that is appropriate for working it through. Conflicts come in all sizes, depths, breadths, and proportions. It is difficult to find or select the proper procedures for dealing with the nature of a particular conflict.

For example, it may be inappropriate for a committee of four to deal with a certain problem that needs full congregational participation. It may be just as inappropriate to unpack certain personal problems in front of a large group, where more damage than good is done.

Responsible discernment calls for understanding the nature of conflict and for skill in devising appropriate procedures for responding to it. We need a combination of practical skills in dealing with conflict, and we need spiritual disciplines for sustaining and guiding those in the pathway of reconciliation.

In summary, the spiritual dimension of "telling it to the church" lies in a basic understanding. The people who make up the church and its very structure are living testimonies of working out the mission of reconciliation (2 Corinthians 5:18-19). The church is a place of encounter. It is a place of Truth-discerning and Truth-telling. It is a place for vulnerable transparency. It is a place for interactive engagement. It is a place of accountability. It is, after all, a place where we journey toward each other and toward God.

STEP 4: RELATE AS WITH A TAX COLLECTOR

This is one of the more complicated aspects of the four steps. It has received no small amount of practice in church history. What does it mean to treat the person with whom you have not been able to reconcile as a "Gentile and tax collector"? Most church members take this as a mandate for avoiding that sinner. It supposedly provides a license to draw the line and separate ourselves. The erring person becomes someone from whom we need distance.

Let us remember that the first three steps have been oriented to moving *toward* conflict and moving *toward* the other. So I pose the question: How would it be consistent for the last step to mean a movement *away* from both?

I do not have a good answer, but I do have a theological method. My understanding of Anabaptist theology has always meant that we are called to be disciples of Jesus. Theologically, what early Anabaptists emphasized was not formulaic dogmas or basic laws. The focus was on following the footsteps of Jesus, an imitation of the behavior and character of Jesus. We are to be centered on Christ, and that is defined largely in terms of action and not simply professed belief.

If we take seriously a theology of following Jesus, then we must let Jesus' actions help us understand the steps he outlined. How did Jesus treat Gentiles and tax collectors? In answering that question, we can discover how we should respond when we reach this stage of conflict. What stands out is this simple answer: Jesus ate with them (as in Matthew 9:10). Time and again, to the chagrin of Pharisees, Jesus chose the route of seeking out and eating with the very people perceived to be impure and outside the believing community. My interpretation of step 4 is this: Eat with them!

"Eating with them" suggests two ideas reflective of what we have seen and what is yet to come in the book:

Across almost all cultures, eating together implies relationship and connection. In the international arena we use *tables* as a metaphor for coming together to talk, negotiate, and seek peace. Eating symbolizes a universal truth that we are connected in the broader human race.

Eating together puts us on the same level. When we are working in complicated international negotiations, eating together often provides a different way for people to connect with and see each other. When we eat together, we are on the same social plane, we admit our sameness, and we recognize our basic humanity. In this sense, eating is a safe space, a place where we are ourselves.

Now connect the act of "eating together" with the earlier steps. As we reach step 4, Jesus' way of operating is fleshed out. Jesus was clear about who he was and how he saw things. Yet he met people, wherever they were, in ways that showed how his love overcame fear. He sought to build relationships, a way of being connected with others. These are precisely the elements noted in the first two steps. They have a parallel to what is now promoted, two thousand years later, in contemporary family systems theory.

Define yourself without projection or retreat. Be clear about who you are. Seek vulnerable transparency. Encourage others to do the same.

Foster a nonanxious presence. Do not get upset, pull back, or be fearful of others when they define themselves differently from you. Interactively engage the difference rather than reacting or trying to control. Move toward the difference and not away from it.

Maintain relational and emotional contact. Stay connected. Eat with each other. In so doing, you will find the reconciliation arts returning to the center—notice mutual humanity, nurture self-reflection, and accompany through committed friendship.

EIGHT

Keep Silent and Listen: *Acts 15*

THE STORY in Acts 15 describes the early church and events surrounding what is often called the Jerusalem Council. Paul and Barnabas have been traveling in foreign territories and sharing the good news of Jesus. They receive a dramatic response and then return to the sending church in Antioch of Syria. After calling the church together, they relate "all that God had done with them, and how he had opened a door of faith for the Gentiles" (Acts 14:27).

However, some folks from Judea arrive and preach to Gentile believers that unless they "are circumcised according to the custom of Moses," they "cannot be saved" (Acts 15:1). The issue produces "no small dissension and debate" between Paul, Barnabas, and the contingent from Judea (Acts 15:2). What, exactly, is "no small dissension"? It might better be depicted as a major church fight, a brouhaha in the pews!

I wish we had video recordings of early church meetings and debates. We carry an image of early church leaders as saints and prophets. Yet if we could see them in action in the everyday life of the local congregation, we would likely be shocked. What we would find most startling is how much they are like us, even having sharp disagreements (as also in Acts 15:39). If we had such a video, we would see and hear things not always readily apparent as we read the text.

We would immediately catch the depth of feeling regarding how critical this issue is for the early church. In our day, the question of circumcision as a requirement for membership may seem remote. What lies behind the debate, however, is the much deeper and more familiar problem: Do we change our beliefs and practices to assimilate what appear to be new ways that God is moving among us?

They are debating the very identity of those who see themselves as the people of God. We would also hear the voices that we often hear today. Most are filled with concern and deep conviction. Each lays claim to the Truth. Some voices are filled with anger, others with fear. A few carry a message of hope.

Many show ambivalence and confusion. They ask, "If this is true, what is God saying to us?" Others hold fast to what is known, to avoid any confusion or ambiguity. They respond, "Our God is a God of order, clarity, and law." I wonder if you have heard such voices in the midst of church debates:

"God is calling us to new understandings of who we are and how we should carry out our mission."

"We have never done it this way. The day you let those people into the church is the day I leave."

"Look right here in the biblical text. It says clearly that we shall not do this."

"Look right here in the biblical text. It shows how this can be done."

Acts 15 is a chapter of conflict. This time we are given a small window into the actual proceedings. How does the early church deal with this problem? Notice again the interplay of practice and spirituality. What steps do they follow? What model does it suggest? What are the assumed spiritual dimensions that undergird such a process?

PRINCIPLES AND STEPS FOR HANDLING CONFLICT

Before we look into the broader principles and steps used in Acts 15, we recall two things from this discussion of context. First, the conflict poses questions central to both theological and churchly concerns. It has to do with identity, organization, and structure. Who are we? What are we called to? How do we organize ourselves in the world? And who makes these decisions? Second, people feel deeply about the issues. Throughout, there are clearly signs of heartfelt emotion. A lot is on the line. With that in mind, let us turn to principles and steps.

1. Recognize and define the problem. The story of Acts 15 is extraordinary because of the forthrightness with which the concerns are raised. They do what is not often done in many church conflicts: They start by acknowledging that they have differences and a conflict. I am always amazed at how long "troubles" can brew before anyone is willing to name them.

I have dealt with many church-related conflicts over the years. Yet I am always surprised at how many people and congregations will first ask for some general education or training about conflict. It often becomes apparent that beneath the request is a decades-long set of dodged issues and concerns that are about to erupt.

This first principle operational in Acts 15 has two different but parallel tracks. It is important to understand that there is a significant difference between knowing and acknowledging. To acknowledge something is to make it explicit, to bring it to the surface, and to recognize it. We are often stuck in a pattern of bumping accidentally into things, going around each other, and circling carefully past the real issues and concerns. This causes confusion and distress. However, we need to openly recognize that we have differences and disagreements that need to be addressed. That step is central to the process of moving forward.

We often fear such acknowledgment. We may fear that, if we openly name the problem, it will damage both our person and our relationship. It will be uncomfortable and painful. The operative base of Acts 15 shows that acknowledging conflict is part of relational transparency and commitment. To disagree does not necessarily have to translate into relational distance and separation. It can mean increased understanding, relationship, and growth.

In my experience, there is once again a paradox: When people fear the step of acknowledgment and avoid it to protect the relationship, those fears often become self-fulfilling. The conflict eventually explodes or implodes. However, if people acknowledge conflict and move toward it early, they find that their relationships can handle even the most difficult of differences.

This paradox lies behind the advice that my colleague Ron Kraybill suggests to congregations: If you want fewer divisive and church-splitting conflicts, encourage more everyday disagreements in congregational life.[5]

It is equally important to work on defining what the conflict is about. Since this is not a how-to manual for dealing with conflict, I will not go into detail about tools and approaches available for defining conflict. As a principle, however, it is important to understand the purpose. Defining what is going on means locating the conflict, what some people call *mapping* the conflict. We want those involved in the conflict to arrive at a common understanding of the nature of the conflict and of what is necessary to work through their concerns.

In international negotiations, this is sometimes called *agenda-building*, which can take years. In church settings, a setting is arranged where people can share their concerns with each other and suggest how those concerns could be handled. Often what

---

5. See Ron Kraybill, *Repairing the Breach: Ministering in Community Conflict* (Scottdale, PA: Herald Press, 1981).

appear to be the hot issues are actually symptoms of other things happening below the surface, things more difficult to name and pinpoint. In Acts 15, people acknowledge and define the specific concerns that need to be addressed.

2. Create the appropriate forum for processing matters. As in Matthew 18, it is necessary to create a forum that fits the needs of the people and the nature of the conflict. This is never an easy task, nor one that appears with ready-made formulas. An orientation toward process is central. How the conflict will be dealt with is of equal or more critical importance than what eventually is decided. Mediator Ron Kraybill once quipped, "Process matters more than outcome." Or as Jim Laue, a mentor of mine, put it, "If you can trust the process, you can trust the outcome."[6]

Matters of process are precisely what must be considered when we talk about creating the proper forum. In Acts 15, an implicit but quite astute process orientation is described, built on discernment and creativity. This is a story of recognizing a conflict that needs broad participation. It moves beyond local congregational experience and toward an inclusive and extended arena.

We note, for example, the dispute between Paul and Barnabas over the travel schedules and participation of John Mark. That creates sharp disagreement. Rather than convening another Jerusalem Council, they part company (Acts 15:36-41). Presumably this conflict is handled at an interpersonal level, though perhaps not very constructively by the standards of Matthew 18 (see the later note of 2 Timothy 4:11).

If we are to take seriously this principle of creating an appropriate forum, several important characteristics identified as *process orientation* need to be outlined. Discernment emerges

---

6. See Jim Laue and Gerald Cormick, "The Ethics of Intervention in Community Disputes," in *The Ethics of Social Intervention*, ed. Gordan Bermat, Herbert Kelman, and Donald Warwick (Washington, DC: Halsted Press, 1979).

from understanding the nature of the conflict and what level of response is needed to deal with it adequately. Creativity is needed for flexibility and innovation.

We must consistently find the mechanisms that hold the greatest potential for helping people understand the concerns and constructively meet each other. This calls for an orientation toward involving people in defining the process. It means finding a forum that feels appropriate and placing a high value on participation and ownership in terms of the substance and the process.

3. Let diverse viewpoints be represented. One of the most striking aspects of the Jerusalem Council is the careful procedure in letting all viewpoints be aired. It is certainly not a meeting of only those who already agree. Instead, this forum gives space for open expression. People share how God has been moving among them and the differences those experiences have highlighted. Significant leaders are present. People who have never ventured out of Jerusalem are there. Paul and Barnabas come, along with other leaders who are emerging as a result of their ministry.

If we return to the process, we find an operational principle of inclusion. Everyone affected by the decision has a place at the table. Acts 15, like Genesis 1 and Matthew 18, speaks to the values of diversity, seeking what God is saying to each person and listening to a voice that can only be fully heard if each is given a place in the choir.

4. Document diversity. In the Acts 15 story, people are given a chance to talk, from Paul and Barnabas to leaders and the people of Jerusalem. In the mediation field, we refer to this as *documenting diversity*. It builds on the prior two principles and provides a space for different voices to be heard. Documenting diversity assumes that people speak and listen.

To speak well and to listen carefully is no easy task at times of high emotions and deep conflict. People's very identity is under threat. I have the impression that it was not easy in the Jerusalem meeting of Acts 15. Again, I wish we had the video, but we don't. We only have a partially told story. Let us fill it in a bit, looking between the lines.

In the title of this chapter, I touched on a short but very crucial line found in Acts 15:12: "The whole assembly kept silence and listened." From the earlier description, I imagine that there has been a period of interaction. The assembly has probably been loud and somewhat confused, with comments flying past responses and counter-responses.

In other words, this is a meeting like our annual session on the church budget. We argue over why so much money is being spent for a new Sunday school wing rather than for refugees in the Horn of Africa. At a given time, the assembly of Acts 15 "kept silence." This stage is qualitatively different from what has preceded, and that is why the writer emphasizes it.

Documenting diversity in the context of the community is about the task of creating a social space for people to speak and listen, and in so doing to hear the voice of God.

5. Use the gifts in the community. As the story weaves on through the meeting, certain people rise and speak. Some bring evidence of what they have seen from their ministry. Some speak of the past. Some speak of how God has worked among them. Some interpret biblical texts. Some formulate ideas of how things will be brought together. Some move the meeting toward a specific outcome. Some write the outcome down. Some carry the message to those not present.

From out of the community come the people and gifts necessary to initiate, support, help create, and sustain the understandings that are reached. This fits Paul's vision of the church as a body (1 Corinthians 12–14). He provides a metaphor of different parts that work together. It is a powerful vision that values diversity and seeks common purpose and understanding. The Acts

15 story describes how that works: the creation of a forum that provides for diversity and seeks common understanding.

6. Decide upon and then implement decisions. One of the more striking aspects of the story is the conclusion. It is striking for what it says and what it does not say. We are told that they reach a conclusion, one that marks from now on the development and expansion of Christianity. It is framed as a compromise decision.

In essence, they decide, "We recognize new things that God has envisioned for the church, things that from our tradition we did not expect. We are changing our beliefs to match this new understanding of God moving among us. However, we recognize important things from our past that we must not let go, and we share them explicitly with our brothers and sisters."

This is a firm move to bring closure to the process. There is no "analysis paralysis" or perpetual process but a specific conclusion that can be implemented.

We are not told what happens at the end of the meeting. I want to know: Does everyone agree with the conclusion? Do they all stay together in harmony? Perhaps some say, "This cannot be. I cannot accept these changes."

We are told that by consent of the body, several leaders are chosen to accompany Paul and Barnabas back to Antioch, to help in reporting the decision of the Jerusalem Council (Acts 15:22-32; see also Acts 21:25). We are not told who, by that time, has left the church in disagreement.

Does engaging in such a process mean consensus is always reached or that there is full agreement and accord? I can hardly

---

Steps for Handling Conflict

1. Recognize and define the problem.

2. Create the appropriate forum for processing matters.

3. Let diverse viewpoints be represented.

4. Document diversity.

5. Use the gifts in the community.

6. Decide upon and then implement decisions.

imagine it. Maybe it has happened in Jerusalem. But I guess that there are probably some—maybe just a minority or maybe more—who do part ways. Paul and Barnabas do part company over Mark. Perhaps they also still disagree about whether it is okay for Jewish Christians to eat with Gentile believers (Acts 15:39, 10:28; Galatians 2:13).

If we take seriously the kind of principles identified in Matthew 18, we understand conflict more clearly. We are called as individuals and congregations to learn the disciplines and skills that help us define ourselves, engage each other in non-anxious interaction, and maintain emotional contact even when we disagree.

If that is truly operative here in Acts 15, one can take this kind of stance: "While I do not agree with where you are going, I will not leave the community and thereby try to force you to adopt my way. Let us agree together to stay in relationship, with each of us seeking to be true to what we sense is our different but deepest calling from God. We may part ways in service, but let us maintain fellowship."

LISTENING: THE SPIRITUAL DIMENSION OF CONFLICT

An important characteristic of dealing with conflict emerges from this story. I will frame it as the spiritual discipline of listening. Beneath the discipline lies a single and most intriguing question: How does God speak to us?

At a technical level, we have often looked at listening in terms of the communication process. One person wants to send a message to another. An intended meaning is thus created that must be conveyed. That meaning is encoded in some fashion, often through words, taking the form of a message. The message must then be perceived by the other person, who decodes it to make sense of it.

Full communication involves the same process in reverse. This purely technical side is already complex. It involves processes of creating, sending, perceiving, and interpreting. If all goes well, what one person means to say is said clearly, and then perceived and interpreted by another in the same way it was intended. That is, we say what we mean, and we understand each other.

We all know that does not always happen, and it certainly becomes much harder to accomplish in the midst of heated conflict. In conflict, before we even hear what the other side has said, we assume we know what they mean. We have already attached motives to their messages. Often, even before they have finished, we are developing our response.

Such dynamics make it difficult to say what we really mean or to hear what the others really mean. We thus create a vicious cycle of misunderstanding and a mutually reinforcing sense of powerlessness. Neither of us feels that we are heard, nor that we say things well. When we do not feel heard, we feel discounted, rejected, and violated. If this continues over time, we are likely to seek ways of making ourselves heard by pushing harder and harder or by retreating for self-protection.

The conflict transformation field teaches that it is necessary to break through this cycle if conflict is to be dealt with constructively. Thus we emphasize the need for listening as an art and a skill. Relying heavily on communication and counseling techniques, a primary approach has been to listen at times of conflict, learning the process of applied paraphrasing, or *active listening.*

Active listening is a practical and useful method. As an applied technique, paraphrasing means to repeat in your own words what another person has said. This changes the dynamics of communication. It slows us down a bit. We check whether what we heard the other person say is what they really meant, and whether what they meant is what we have understood. We show the other that we are truly interested in understanding them and in being understood.

Instead of relying on instinct and gut reaction, in paraphrasing we actively try to break out of the cycle of miscommunication. We must first make sure we have understood each other before we try to deal with our differences.

I have monitored this process. When paraphrasing is a natural part of a person's repertoire of skills and when it is done well, it goes virtually unperceived. People want to be heard and are often grateful that somebody cares enough to interact constructively with what they are saying.

However, I have also found that when we teach the skill in seminars, there is some reaction against the technical skill. People dislike any formulaic crutch that becomes part of the technique: "What I hear you saying is . . ." It makes the process sound fake. People react against being submitted to a form of gratuitous parroting or cheap "psychologizing."

This reaction leads to an insight that helps us connect to a deeper level. What really bothers people is the perception of underlying purpose and attitude. The technique is merely a tool. It can be used for good or bad. What counts is intuited beneath the technique: the quality and nature of one's spirit. True listening is connected to a spiritual process. Consider three different but related facets of this deeper process.

Listening is a spiritual discipline. Listening as a technique takes art and skill. To apply the technique takes discipline. But such technical discipline, even if well honed in the helping professions, does not in itself lead to a deeper level of genuine listening. I can use the technique, for example, to simply get information about you. What leads to the deeper level is whether I interact with you as a person about whom I care.

To use a more biblical term, listening is a spiritual discipline if, like a spring, it bubbles up from genuine love. I refer to love in the sense of *agape*, a self-sacrificing love, which today is better understood as true caring. I take care in my relationship with you. I care about your experience and journey. I care about you as a person. This involves personal risk. In actively caring and seeking to truly interact with you, my experience and journey will be affected, shaped, and molded. I will learn something of you and something of me.

Listening is like prayer. Now add a second intriguing idea. The pursuit of listening as a spiritual discipline calls for reframing what we are doing when we listen. Reframing is based on the idea that we create meaning when we associate things together, and different associations provide different meanings.[7]

I have often used my son's response to "babysitting" as an example. When his older sister Angie was in school, Joshua was dropped off a few hours a week at a neighbor's house. He was negative about the experience. If we referred to this as "going to the babysitter's place," he rebelled. Babysitting meant being left out, going to a stranger's house, or whatever image was conjured up in his four-year-old mind.

To deal with his resistance, we tried referring to this time and place as "school," and to the babysitter as a teacher. Then Joshua associated it with what his big sister was doing, and he was content. It had a positive meaning. The same thing meant something different because of its different connections.

The same is true of listening. Much of what is technically taught about listening is associated with professional fields. We have, I think, relied on a narrow and unnecessarily superficial association. It therefore is not surprising that we understand listening primarily as a technique. I believe prayer is the closest biblical and spiritual phenomenon to listening. The purpose of this chapter is not to explore and fully unpack all that might be meant by prayer. However, there are a number of characteristics to consider, particularly in the context of thinking about conflict and reconciliation.

---

7. See Paul Watzlawick, et al., *Change: Principles of Problem Formation and Problem Resolution* (New York: Norton, 1974).

I understand prayer to involve a relationship and conversation with God. It is ongoing. I take what occupies my mind and heart, and I seek to learn what God has for me. The latter can only be discovered through a process of learning. I must bracket the many noises and rumblings that float through my mind and my busy day. I do this so I can focus and make it possible for God's voice to enter and speak, and for me to recognize God's voice.

This involves an attitude of attentive awareness and a discipline. In attentive awareness, I pay attention and look for the presence of God in what may appear to be the most mundane of things. Discipline implies that it takes consistent willingness. I must care about doing it or it doesn't happen.

The desire for relationship and love supports attentive awareness and discipline. Prayer is not so much about words or formulas. Prayer is attentive awareness and discipline based on relationship and love. This combination creates the space for interaction, transparency, and understanding. When we practice these things, we are truly listening.

Listening is seeking God. The idea of prayer and listening as a spiritual discipline leads to the discovery that to truly listen is to seek God. This is rather astonishing, given that we are exploring the context of how we understand conflict. Situations of conflict are often filled with noise and periods of deep, silent distance. How is it possible in these situations to find God? How can listening to my enemy be understood as sacred? It involves at least a twofold process.

First, from earlier discussions in Genesis, I begin with a view that there is "that of God" in every human being (see chapter 2). Second, God moves and speaks to each of us, whether we are aware of it or not. This leads to a simple but profound conclusion. We provide the space to listen to another and genuinely try to understand. Thus we are helping to create the opportunity for that person and for ourselves to get in touch with what God may be saying and what God is trying to do in the present.

I have referred to this as "prophetic listening," a concept I first heard from Elise Boulding. During conflicts, many prophets speak and often quite loudly. People lay claim to the Truth as if it were theirs alone. Few prophets listen. Prophetic listening, as I see it, is the discipline of listening with others in such a way that it helps them get in touch with what God is telling them (cf. 1 Corinthians 14:29; 1 Thessalonians 5:20-21).

In this sense, prophetic listening is like going on a journey alongside the person to whom we are listening. This kind of listening does what few other things can do. It helps us feel the presence and direction of God's truth.

IMPLICATIONS FOR CHURCHES

All of this has profound implications for how to think about and respond to conflict at all levels, but especially for church-related dissension and debate, large or small. When we understand listening as a spiritual discipline, as prayer, and as seeking God, then we recognize that God speaks to us through others.

Our capacity to listen to God is only as great as our capacity to listen to each other when we are in conflict. I mean that literally. We test our real capability to listen, not when it is easy, but when it is most difficult. Listening is much more than a technique devised to improve communication. Listening is about the process of relationship, engaging Truth, and finding God.

The churchly importance embedded in Acts 15 cannot be overstated. The procedures of Acts 15 give us a vision that the beloved community is not a static outcome of our work. It is a dynamic process of interaction and growth. Conflict is not and cannot be seen as a disruption in our otherwise peaceful life. Conflict provides an arena for revelation.

Reconciliation is understood as both a place we are trying to reach and the journey that we take up with each other. The window of Acts 15 gives a living model of this idea. Conflict provides an arena for God to speak. This can happen as we understand listening to be a spiritual discipline, like prayer, and place ourselves on the journey of seeking God together.

NINE

Reconciliation *Is* the Gospel: *Paul's Letters*

W HEN I WORKED at a Mennonite college, one of my colleagues told me about a conversation he had with several members of a Mennonite congregation. They had asked, "When will the Mennonite church and its academic centers stop fussing so much about peace issues and get on with the gospel?"

"How would you answer these genuine concerns?" my colleague wanted to know. He waited for my answer.

"I may not be a good person to ask," I replied, knowing that my answer is not one that these sisters and brothers would want to hear.

"My first response is this: reconciliation *is* the gospel."

THE PURPOSE OF GOD'S MISSION

In earlier chapters and through a variety of stories, I have said that reconciliation is a journey. On this journey we encounter God, others, and ourselves. Such a journey, I believe, is the essence of the gospel. It lies at the heart of God's intention for humanity and with humanity.

In Christian circles, we have too often assumed that reconciliation is an outgrowth, a side benefit that emerges from the core of individual faith, confession, and conversion. In this view, reconciliation is a product of proper belief. However, I maintain that reconciliation is better understood as a journey.

But an understanding of reconciliation as a journey will require us to adjust our thinking and activity. To see reconciliation as a journey and not a byproduct means that reconciliation is central, a defining model of who and how God is in the world.

I view reconciliation as the mission, the organizing purpose around which we understand and see God's work in history. I believe that the way God has chosen to be present and act throughout history demonstrates a methodology of reconciliation. Our mission is to align ourselves with God, who is working to bring all things together, to reconcile all of creation—particularly a broken, estranged humanity. This is the "universal restoration" destined to bless all families of the earth (Acts 3:20-26; Colossians 1:20).

The methodology is how God's mission is made present in our world: it happens through the incarnation, the way in which Word becomes flesh. This is why building peace, justice, and reconciliation is not a sideshow interest for a few. Reconciliation is getting to the heart of the gospel and getting on with the gospel.

Here I reflect on the nature of this journey and the quality of God's love. I will work with the Pauline vision of Christ, who through the cross has brought all things together.

ALL THINGS COME TOGETHER

In the letter to the Colossians, Paul writes that through Christ, God was pleased to reconcile all things to himself and that in Christ all things are held together (Colossians 1:17, 20). To the Ephesians, he writes that through the cross, Christ has broken down the dividing wall of hostility and created in himself a new humanity that is reconciled with each other and God (Ephesians 2:13-14).

We have generally understood this language as a theological treatise about atonement, which then leads to a holy life. We tend to see atonement as an act of sacrifice whereby Jesus' death on the cross satisfies our debt of sin in front of God our Creator. As such, atonement is understood as a ritualistic act of cleansing, often individualized to the relationship between a person and God: through the blood of Christ on the cross, an indebted, sinful person is reconciled to God. Holiness then apparently means keeping ourselves pure, at some distance from whatever is messy, evil, and sinful.

Ironically, this construct lends itself to a narrow understanding not only of atonement and holiness but of the very nature of God's mission. Let us expand our view by using the bold and venturesome vision of Paul. He states in simple terms that God's purpose and mission is to bring all things together. This is a vision of reconciliation. It lies at the heart of the good news. God moves toward us to mend and heal what has been torn apart. God's mission is reconciliation.

As a point of departure and reference, this vision changes our understanding of atonement and holiness. It provokes us to reassess and develop a more challenging way of thinking about mission, our place in the world, and our part in the work of God in history.

In the Pauline vision, atonement does not simply mean a sacrifice that satisfies an individual debt. There is a greater emphasis on atonement as a personal, social, and political process of reconciliation and healing. Holiness is not driven by a concern for boundaries that protect purity. Instead, holiness is carried out through people who embody the reconciling love of God and take up residence in real-life problems and relationships, with all the ambiguities they bring.

A NEW HUMANITY

Let us explore this vision in more detail by reconsidering Ephesians 2:11-22 with the lens of reconciliation as mission placed over our eyes. Paul describes two peoples who have been divided and estranged. And then he writes,

> But now in Christ Jesus you who once were far off have been brought near by the blood of Christ. For he is our peace; in his flesh he has made both groups into one and has broken down the dividing wall, that is, the hostility between us. He has abolished the law with its commandments and ordinances, that he might create in himself one new humanity in place of the two, thus making peace, and might reconcile both groups to God in one body through the cross, thus putting to death that hostility through it. (Ephesians 2:13-16)

Paul starts with a reference to peoples who are separated, enemies, distant, strangers who stand apart. Through Christ, however, the dividing wall of hostility has been broken down. In Christ, those who once were enemies are now reconciled in a new, single humanity. I note here two qualities, neither of which is particularly ritualistic or symbolic. On the contrary, they are rather literal and organic.

First, Paul makes reference throughout the text to peoples who are enemies. The context to which he refers is that of the Jews and Gentiles, enemy peoples not unlike the Hutus and Tutsis of Rwanda, the First Nations and the Americans of European descent, or the Christians and Muslims in Nigeria. These are people who have hurt and killed each other, whose identities are sharply divided by a sense of threat, injustice, and separation. Throughout the text, these are referred to as groups and not as individuals. The concluding reconciliation creates a new humanity by bringing the groups together.

In this text, atonement is literally about a dynamic group process, a journey where real enemies with deep hostilities are reconciled. Organically, Christ plows soil where seeds and roots of hatred have been born and fed for centuries. Joe Campbell, my good colleague from Northern Ireland, commented, "We must tend to our soil that produces the bitterness and anger." This is simultaneously a personal, social, and political process. It is not, however, merely an individualistic event.

Second, Paul depicts Christ as a person through whom new relationships are formed. Again I am struck with the literal and organic nature of this description. In the life of Jesus, holiness is defined more than anything else by his persistent movement toward people, their pain, and the formation of a new relationship.

In this text, Paul declares that through Christ, through a person who reaches out across lines of hostility, through his very flesh and person, enemies meet and are held together. Thus they form a new humanity, a new relationship. What we find here is the most necessary part of the mission methodology: movement into relationship.

From the perspective of God's purpose, the example of Christ Jesus is clear. It is not possible to pursue reconciliation except through people who risk the journey to relate across the social divides. In this way they help make present the reconciling love of God. In other words, through people who reach across the lines of hostility, a new relationship between enemies becomes possible.

RECONCILIATION RATHER THAN PURITY

Over past centuries, some Christians, including Mennonites, my home denomination, have chosen to embody atonement and holiness by the motto "We are in the world but not of the world" (see John 17:11, 16 KJV). We use this text to support notions of nonconformity. We say this means that we choose not to live conformed to the pressures around us but rather by the standards and ethics of the kingdom of God (see also Romans 12:2).

In practice, this has often been applied as removing ourselves from the world, pulling back, and isolating our communities from the world. Because of our concern for holiness, we try to control the environment around us so that we will have less opportunity to fall and fail. In our practice we have placed the emphasis on the "not of the world" portion of the motto.

Ironically, God through Jesus seems to have approached holiness and atonement with an emphasis on the "in the world" part of the motto. The world is a messy, violent, and broken place. God's model child, Jesus, was needed in the world to provide the distinctive direction. This would be something different from the way people were acting and carrying on. By God's example through Jesus, "to be in but not of the world" means that we move *toward* human troubles and choose to live in the messiness. That way the alternative of God's reconciling love can be made known.

From such a view, atonement and holiness are not about establishing proper ritual and merely maintaining individual purity. Atonement and holiness are about entering relationships and starting dynamic social processes that help create the space for a new humanity to emerge. We choose to journey toward and with those who have experienced the deepest division and separation because this is God's mission and Christ's example.

TRUE ATONEMENT

I believe the Pauline vision leads us to a simple but challenging conclusion: God is working to bring all things together. The purpose is to heal and to reconcile people with each other and with God. God's mission is also ours. We have been given the same ministry of reconciliation (2 Corinthians 5:18-20).

This ministry, as articulated by Paul, is not just about individual salvation. It is about facing divisions and restoring people in their relationships with others and with God. It is about joining God in the mission of reconciliation by building bridges and bringing down the dividing walls of hostility between individuals and groups.

True atonement and holiness place us on the journey to make real the reconciling love of God in our lives and to heal our broken communities across the globe. Our mission is to walk the path by which all things come together.

PEDRITO'S DREAM

We are living in a period of fast changes, at the beginning of a new century that has already given us great promise, challenge, and pain.

At various moments, such as when the Berlin Wall literally fell and the nonviolent actions of the Arab Spring occurred, we have asked, "Is the dream of peace actually possible?" At times there has been a sense of promise and celebration. We can all feel the words of poet Robert Frost stirring within us: "Something there is that doesn't love a wall." Maybe peace is not a utopian dream, we think in these times.

Yet at other times, as during the Gulf War, September 11, the invasion of Afghanistan, and the killings in Rwanda and Syria, we experience the unleashing of unfathomable violence. Flashing across our televisions and newspapers, we stand, almost dumbfounded, as the death machine with its modern flamboyance, sheer power, and advanced technology capture our unbelieving eyes and imagination. "What happened to the dream of peace?" we manage to stutter to each other, our voices drowned out in the din of war-making. We hear cries for victory and support for our troops in atonement for past failures. We fall almost deathly silent, our dream of peace unreal and invalidated. We watch untold atrocities unfold in Somalia, Rwanda, Afghanistan, the Democratic Republic of the Congo, Syria, and in our own towns and cities—violence that numbs our senses and leaves us feeling paralyzed. These are difficult times for dreams.

I am reminded of close friends in Nicaragua. We held a workshop with some key leaders in local and regional peace commissions originally formed under the Central American peace plan. During our time together, my friends started telling stories of their mediation work. One was Pedrito.

Though Pedrito had little formal education, he was an elected leader of a cooperative movement representing more than two thousand *campesinos*. He talked about the complications and difficulties of traveling by foot or horseback more than five days into the mountains. He was seeking out people who were still armed. He would build bridges with them and encourage them to come down and meet their enemies face-to-face. Then he would trek five days back by foot to meet with the government and army officials and to encourage them to meet leaders of these opposition forces.

I asked my friends why they took on these dangerous tasks. Pedrito simply answered, "We all want peace. We, we who are bearers of the good news, have been given the ministry of reconciliation. It is our job, our responsibility."

One afternoon we lunched in the hot Managua sun. Pedrito had asked the maintenance people at the hotel for a sack. He was filling it with big seed pods that were falling on the veranda from a huge Guanacaste tree overhead. I asked him what he was doing, and he said, "We have a problem with deforestation in my area. I want to take back these seeds for the people. Nobody here really seems to want them."

I will remember the image of Pedrito walking toward his bus stop with his huge white sack of Guanacaste seeds on his back. This was a symbolic sack of dreams for his people. It embodied the ministry of reconciliation that not only bridges human conflict but cares and gives back to the creation what God has provided. The harvest of justice, we are told, is sown in peace by those who make peace (James 3:18 CEV).

Pedrito is a dreamer. He has his feet grounded in the realities of his native Nicaragua and his head in the clouds. Day in and out, he is living by a dream that things can be different. Each of us needs our own big sack of Guanacaste seeds, our sack of dreams that we carry on our way.

SAM DOE'S DREAM

Several years ago I had the great privilege of working, teaching, and learning from Sam Doe. Sam is from Liberia, where he has toiled the ground of peacebuilding during the many long years of ethnic fighting and violence. He told me the story of how he came to work with child soldiers that have been so common in the Liberian war.

Sam initiated a number of workshops with the Christian Health Association of Liberia. They began to work with young children who had been fighters for one faction or other in the war. Sam tells of one young man by the name of Korte. He had been taken at a young age into the ranks of the fighters. When they were inducted at ages nine to twelve, they were often sent back into the very areas and villages they came from, with a mission to destroy everything that was there.

The warlords assigned the boys to commit such atrocious acts to create loyalty in their hearts and minds. Afterward, the boys attached their security, lives, and futures to the local militias. At age ten, Korte was changed in such a way.

When Sam met him, he was in a refugee encampment and experiencing hallucinations from his recent violent experiences and the steady flow of drugs he had been fed. Sam worked with him day in and day out. Korte would have visual and aural visions that pushed him to violence. He would say that his grandmother was calling him to do these things. Sam told him that whenever Korte had a vision, he should come to Sam. On numerous occasions, Sam had to deal with violent confrontations and bring Korte back to real life.

One day, however, Sam needed to leave for a week in neighboring Ivory Coast. When he returned a week later, his colleagues told him that Korte was dead. Just a few days earlier, Korte had come to the office with bad hallucinations. Claiming that he was a prince, the son of the King of the Coast, he said his father was calling him home. Within a few hours, he had walked into the salty tide of a nearby beach and drowned. At sixteen, after carrying a gun in a war of adults for six years, Korte was dead.

Sam was devastated. He recalls going straight home from the office. After a few hours at home, he walked out to the beach where only days before Korte had committed suicide. There Sam found himself struggling with a deep sense of anger and despair. At first he was angry with his colleagues. "Why?" he heard himself nearly shouting at them as if they were there. "Why did you not do something to stop him?"

He was also angry at himself. "Why did I even go to Ivory Coast? Why didn't I stay home?"

Then he found himself addressing God. "Why did you create a small boy and let him fall into the hands of such violence and evil? Where were you when Korte needed you most?"

Sam says he waded for hours along the shore, between tears of sadness and tears of anger. After that long afternoon, he arose with a new conviction, one that would carry him through his next hours and days, years, and a lifetime. "I will give my life to working with child soldiers, making sure this madness of violence does not destroy our country."

From the first time I met Sam, he has always talked about his dream—the dream that one day justice, peace, and reconciliation would root themselves and grow in Liberia. Since then, Sam has traveled all over West Africa and in his native Liberia, giving seminars on peacebuilding, trauma healing, and working with child soldiers. That day at the beach, the seeds of a dream were born from the waters of despair and harsh reality.

Sam has his feet deep in his native soil, a soil drenched with too much blood and suffering. He has his head in the clouds, believing so firmly that reconciliation is possible that he has chosen to give his whole life to making it come true.

Are we not all faced with the same questions that face Sam? What dreams do we people of faith have? Is not the dream of reconciliation a real possibility, where all things are brought together? Cannot our dreams and convictions have the power of transformation in the face of today's real challenges? Are these not the dreams of our Creator? What kind of God do we believe in?

DREAMS OF RECONCILIATION

I believe in the God of history, the God of creation, the God of love and compassion, the God of immeasurable power. This God has chosen to work through the weak and foolish. To rescue enemies, this God chose to give away a child, the beloved Son, the one most cherished.

I believe in a God who, like a mother or a father, sees and cares for each child on this earth through the eyes of a parent and not through the eyes of nationality. This parent weeps at the pain and death that some children inflict on others.

I believe in the God of shalom, who invites us to be a part of the new kingdom dream. There human energies are spent on healing the sick, housing the homeless, and feeding the hungry. There we choose not the weapons of destruction to resolve our differences but the God-given gifts of reason and speech and the overwhelming coals of love and compassion (see Romans 12:20).

I believe justice, peace, and reconciliation are possible. I believe they will happen.

The journey toward reconciliation calls us to embrace the paradox. Caught as we are between the realities we see around us and the dreams we have, we must not choose one over the other. To move toward reconciliation, we must keep our feet on the ground, connected to the pulse of real-life challenges, and our heads in the clouds, with a dream that things can be different.

In Colombia they have a saying: "You must be so close to the ground that you can hear the grass grow." This is our challenge: to stay so close to the ground that we feel the very soil's moisture bubbling up from people's daily life, pains, and realities. Yet we must be so close to our dreams of what could be that we can feel and hear the seeds pregnant with life as they break forth from below the surface.

Faith beckons us to join the cloud of witnesses. We are invited to join people having a practical commitment to face the challenges of their day, and simultaneously, the courage to dream about what could and should be.

More than fifty years ago, the voice of Martin Luther King Jr. thundered out the simple words, "I have a dream." That speech stands out, not only for his call to racial equality and justice, but for his simple audacity to dream.

To take up the journey of reconciliation, we keep our feet on the ground and our head in the clouds. Now is the time for great convictions and great dreams. Let us dream boldly. Let us dream boldly, that our feet may carry us through the challenging realities that stir around us.

May God grant us the innocence to dream and the wisdom, courage, and sustenance to take up the journey.

Resources

TOOLS FOR UNDERSTANDING CONFLICT

INTERPERSONAL CONFLICT: PATTERNS

Carolyn Schrock-Shenk

People develop particular patterns of engaging conflict. Consider the spectrum below, and then address the questions following the spectrum. These patterns can also be used as windows into the systemic nature of most conflicts.

0 1 2 3	4 5 6	7 8 9 10
Fears or dislikes conflict	**Accepts conflict as normal**	**Sees conflict as contest**
Runs and/or hides	Inviting and engaging	Plunges in
Avoids or gives in	Listens to understand	Listens in order to counter or trap
Seeks not to hurt or get hurt	Committed to mutuality	Argumentative/overbearing
Can be passive aggressive	No need to win	Winning is crucial
Relationship matters most	Relationship *and* issue matter	Issue/perspective matters more than relationship
Hands: crossed over chest	Hands: out with palms up	Hands: fists

1. What number best describes your pattern of conflict in each of these contexts?

    a. With your peers ____

    b. With your family ____

    c. In your workplace ____

    d. In your congregation ____

2. In each case, to what do you attribute the development of this particular pattern? (Culture, tradition, personality, biblical understanding, etc.)

3. Would you like to change any of these patterns? If so, which ones? What are some ways you might be able to accomplish the changes?

INTERPERSONAL CONFLICT:
CENTERED COMMUNICATION

Carolyn Schrock-Shenk

Centered communication is a combination of centered speaking, *providing information about what is happening at the center of ourselves, and* centered listening, *tuning in to the heart of the other. Below are some attributes of each.*

Understandings about Centered Speaking

- Uncentered speaking is full of *you, you, you* (blame and judgment).

- Centered speaking focuses on vulnerable information about *me*: my emotions, needs, fears, preferences, and the impact of a situation (or your actions) on me.

- Centered speaking acknowledges and keeps the focus on *my* responsibility.

- Centered speaking does not excuse my behavior by blaming it on the behavior of others.

- Centered speaking involves centered listening to myself—my center, my heart—and then speaking from that place.

Principles of Centered Listening in Conflict

- Attitude—specifically an attitude of curiosity, humility, and openness to change—is much more important than skills.

- Understanding is not about agreement but about respect—including respect of the other's right to a perspective *different* from mine.

- Listen loosely to the words, tightly to the meaning: What is the essence of the other's message?

- Centered listening means accepting that I have only part of the truth in every situation (only God sees the whole; I see "through a glass dimly").

- The other person or group will usually be ready to listen after (and only after) being heard and understood.

INTERPERSONAL CONFLICT:
CONFRONTING AND PROBLEM-SOLVING
Carolyn Schrock-Shenk

Below are some points to remember when confronting some-one in a conflict and when trying to solve a problem with someone who has a different perspective or opinion.

Confronting

- Be sure the issue is worth confronting. Some things just need to be accepted. Confront if you care enough about *both* the *issue* and the *relationship*.

- Plan the setting. Find an appropriate time and place.

- Plan the wording, using centered communication principles.

  - Be clear about the issue; present it without evaluation or judgment.

  - Describe your feelings and the impact of the issue or situation on you.

  - Explain why it matters (unmet needs and expectations).

  - Clearly express what you want or need in the form of a request rather than a demand.

- Be intentional about your nonverbal messages. Be assertive, not aggressive or passive. Passion and strong feelings are natural, but being too passionate or forceful can be intimidating and is usually counterproductive.

Problem Solving

1. **Share perspectives.** As each party shares her or his perspective of the situation or issue, the other person listens to

understand (not trap) and then paraphrases. Each person needs to be heard and understood.

2. **Identify issues and interests.** Identify and agree on the key issues and the interests that lie under each of them. What is the conflict actually about and why does it matter to you?

3. **Identify options for each issue.** Be creative; think outside the box. There are always more than two options.

4. **Negotiate.** Which option best addresses the interests and satisfies both of you? Win/win? Compromise? Agree to disagree?

5. **Closure and follow-up.** In some way, reaffirm the relationship as you part and agree to check in with each other.

Carolyn Schrock-Shenk is associate professor of peace, justice, and conflict studies at Goshen College in Goshen, Indiana. She thanks many others who came before her for contributing to these resources.

CHURCH CONFLICT:
THE UNSPOKEN COMMANDMENTS

John Paul Lederach

During years of consulting, I have found that the most common view of conflict in church circles is that conflict is sin. In this way of thinking, conflict demonstrates that people are falling from the straight and narrow way. Working with and through conflict is essentially a matter of making sure people "get right with God."

My experiences have led me to question this rather spiritualized view and to appreciate a different biblical and theological understanding of conflict. Typically, we have not looked into conflict as a theological issue to be explored. Usually we simply count a party in opposition to "our group" to be also in opposition to God.

When faced with conflict, many of us in the church operate by a series of understood but unexpressed rules and guidelines. I call them the "Unspoken Ten Commandments of Conflict in the Church." The Unspoken Commandments are not exclusive to church circles; social scientists would suggest that they are rooted in a series of common dynamics that accompany conflict as it escalates.

Unspoken Ten Commandments of Conflict in the Church

1. **Thou shalt be nice.** Always be nice. Yea, I say unto thee, "niceness" is the essence of Christianity.

2. **Thou shalt not confront each other in public.** Confrontation is nasty and unmanageable. If ever in doubt about confrontation, refer to commandment number one.

3. **Should thou ever have the distasteful experience of confrontation, thou shalt not listen to thine enemy, but shalt prepare thy defense while the enemy is still speaking.**

Yea, I say unto thee, listening raises questions that weaken thy defense and may lead to compromise, impurity, and, heaven forbid, self-reflection. It is dangerous to change thy mind or admit that thou wert wrong. Truth is unchangeable.

4. **Speak not with contentious folks who disagree with thee or who have raised thy "righteous" anger.** Thou shalt seek out and talk to others about them. Yea, more, dear brothers and sisters, speak only with nice people who agree with thee. By speaking only with those with whom thou dost agree, thou wilt experience the true support of community.

5. **Remember that thou art of noble and decent character, and thou shalt not show thine emotions in public.**

6. **Men, be rational.** Do not show weakness through emotions like crying or anger. It is better for thee to disengage from a situation of conflict and remain silent than to show uncontrolled emotion.

7. **Women, thou shalt not defend thyself vigorously, nor "nag" incessantly, or they may call thee the dreaded B-word.** Thou shalt be prepared to have thine opinions ignored, realizing that those same opinions may be accepted as valid if later stated by a man. Thou shalt not gripe about this in the presence of men.

8. **If thou dost not like the way things are going in the church, thou shalt blame the pastor.** Most problems can be traced to the pastor. If the pastor is a saint, then blame the church council. If the church council is clean, then blame "them." Keep it a generic and undefined "they" or "some people I know." If thou cannot find anyone to blame, leave the church. Verily, I say, a church where there is nobody to blame is not worth staying in.

9. **If thou must confront, save thine energy, frustration, and irritation for the annual budget meeting.** God gave annual budget meetings to bring congregational catharsis.

10. **Dear Christian sisters and brothers, in a holy nutshell I say unto ye all, thou shalt not have conflict in the church.** Conflict is a sign of sin. Yea, should conflict emerge, pray that God may convict and convert thine erring enemies.

This list looks with humor at our behavior, but I believe these Unspoken Commandments describe many people's experiences. Such patterns may even come too close for comfort. In part, that is because these commandments connect with some typical responses that form the underpinnings, not of what we say we believe, but of what we actually do with conflict. What we actually do is our practice, or praxis.

Conflict is painful and messy. We may deal with the uncertainty of messiness on a theological level by suggesting that conflict is primarily a question of sin, "their" sin. At a personal level, we deal with the pain and anxiety by finding a variety of clever ways to avoid facing the conflict. We find justifications for moving away from rather than toward conflict. Too often we adjust our theology to match what we actually do. To support avoidance, we cite biblical clauses, using them detached from their context: "Have nothing more to do with anyone who causes divisions" (Titus 3:10).

CHURCH CONFLICT:
CHANGES THAT CONFLICT CAN PRODUCE

John Paul Lederach

Conflict changes things. It transforms perceptions, communication, relationships, and the structure and organization of groups. Conflict can also be painful and threatening. The worst expressions of hostility can be psychologically damaging and physically violent. We usually do everything possible to avoid it.

Several sociological patterns create common outcomes if they are carried on unabated. As conflict escalates, people tend to distrust and move away from those who are perceived to hold different views or are creating the discomfort. There is less direct and accurate communication.

Consider some of the more important changes that conflict can produce.

Change 1: The other person becomes the problem.

When we are in a healthy relationship, we are able to do several things well as we face differences and disagreements. We can acknowledge openly that a conflict exists. We share responsibility for facing it. We work together on the issues.

However, when the argument heats up or when we feel questioned or threatened, our defenses go up, and a first change sets in. Rather than sharing responsibility for the problems with the other person, we begin to see the other person as the problem.

This simple change is subtle but lies at the root of how conflict can move in divisive and destructive directions. If we primarily or exclusively operate with the idea that the other person is the problem, the solutions are to change the person, to get away from the person, or in the worst scenario, to get rid of the person.

Too often we see conflict as a battle to be won instead of a problem to be addressed in the relationship. We think that if we eliminate the person, we eliminate the problem. This viewpoint starts with the first common shift in the early stage of conflict: seeing the other person as the problem.

Change 2: Issues multiply.

The second major change is what happens to the issues. Have you noticed what pops into your mind when somebody confronts you? "Yeah, and what makes you such a saint? Why, just last week I saw you . . ."

Suddenly you raise a different issue that shifts attention away from the questions your friend has just posed. She may then counter by adding another concern that bothers her. The discussion feels confused and tangled. You both move from one topic to the next, without conclusion or clarity.

Issues multiply. This is common as conflict progresses. We pull in more issues. We can easily feel overwhelmed and unclear about what, exactly, this conflict is about.

One central tension in many conflicts is which, of the many issues, is the real problem. This may be why we describe conflict as a "mess" or "a can of worms," where creepy and slimy things just keep crawling out. Many people respond to conflict with simple advice: "Don't open that can. Avoid the messy confusion."

Change 3: Language changes.

A third dynamic is the way our language changes as conflict escalates. Because we see the other person as the threat, we begin to project blame onto "you." Pay attention to how the accusing and even finger-pointing form of "you" increases as people get angrier and more intensely involved in the conflict. "You are so irritating." "You make me so angry."

Along with projecting blame, our language tends to become more generalized as conflict escalates. We talk in less specific terms about the issues and the people. We stereotype by saying "they." We put people in a unit and describe them in broad, general strokes. For example: "Well, you know, that's just how those charismatics are."

It's always easier to maintain a defensive stance about the other side when we operate with stereotypes and generalizations. As issues increase and language gets more general, people are less sure of what is really going on and how to respond. At the same time, they feel increasingly threatened and defensive.

Change 4: Talk with like-minded people increases.

A fourth major change begins as we talk with like-minded persons about our problems and conflicts. This is natural to all groups and societies, though it takes different forms. Instead of talking directly with the people with whom we have the problem, we talk to others about them.

In church settings, this dynamic is in line with several of our Unspoken Commandments. As tensions escalate, we tend to move away from discussion of controversial issues and away from those who do not agree with us. We move toward friends who agree with us. We are nice in public, but we talk behind the backs of others because we do not have the skill or the will to address our differences directly. In other words, we stoop to backbiting (Romans 1:30; 2 Corinthians 12:20 KJV).

Change 5: Focus moves from original issue to most recent action.

A fifth dimension changes the nature of our response. We respond to the situation according to the latest "thing" that "the other side" has done. We focus on responding to their latest action or comment. The conflict moves away from originating and core issues. The pattern sets in motion a cycle of action-reaction that operates almost on its own energy.

This can be accompanied by a change in goals, though we rarely discuss our goals openly. In the worst settings, people move from feeling personal antagonism toward more direct forms of hostility. In some cases, these may be open forms of violence. In others, the expressions of hostility may be indirect, as in psychological warfare.

Our initial goal was to understand the issues and each other. Our new goal is to win, get revenge, and do harm to the other. Everyone involved experiences a deep and real sense of threat that produces insecurity and doubts about ourselves.

Change 6: Middle ground disappears.

Eventually, conflict can change the social organization of a group. The process of "moving away" is no longer just an individual thing. Often the original group splits into two opposing groups. People feel pressure to be on one side or the other: "You are either with us or against us." Sides form as clear groups emerge. There is almost no middle ground.

Some who are thought of as extremists at an early stage later become leaders. Communication patterns change. When conflict is fully escalated, people tend to talk only with those who agree with them. They have little contact with differing viewpoints. Consequently, each group is increasingly dependent on indirect information about what others are thinking. There is less accurate communication.

CHURCH CONFLICT: DECLARATIONS

John Paul Lederach

A number of important assertions about conflict and how to respond to it emerge from the material in this book. Here is a short list of declarations, some descriptive and some directive.

1. Conflict is a part of the church.

What is perhaps most astonishing about the four steps outlined by Jesus in Matthew 18 is not what he said, but what he assumes and does not say. Jesus simply assumes that in the life of the church, as in the life of any relationship, there will be times of disagreement, conflict, and interpersonal and group clashes.

Jesus moves straight ahead to provide procedure for what we should do as this happens. In this way, Matthew 18 reinforces the creation commitments in Genesis 1. Jesus follows a line already established. He assumes the dynamic but often painful understanding that conflict is a part of human relationships and a part of church life.

2. Move toward conflict.

What underlies the four steps throughout the Matthew 18 text is Jesus' invitation to move toward the source of our anxiety and toward conflict itself. We have a tendency in church circles to see conflict as messy, as "unchristian." We somehow carry an image that the church is a place made up of saints, or at least nice people who do not experience this kind of messiness.

We often set up ourselves to experience a superficial understanding of each other and little positive interaction around our differences. We begin to think that being in church means that we all agree, but the opposite is true.

The church, like the human family, should be a place where members value diversity, encourage honest expression of disagreements, and see relationships as possible between those who do not agree. The church is the place of reconciliation, where conflict is understood as necessary and important for learning and growth. That can happen only as we capture an understanding and vision that moves us toward conflict, not away from it.

3. Move toward the other.

Jesus challenges us to examine how we view those with whom we experience conflict and deeply felt differences. What consistently underlies the four steps is his call for us to move toward the other rather than away from him or her. We need to cultivate practical skills for confronting each other in better ways. We also need to develop a spiritual discipline through which we seek interactive engagement with others and God.

4. The church is a forum for expressing and handling conflict.

Jesus provides overall guidelines in this teaching. The church as envisioned here is not simply a glee club of harmonious voices. It is a place to interact with each other, express differences, and work through what may be painful theological and relational issues and concerns. The church is a forum for expressing and dealing with conflict. What is needed is both the vision of integrating conflict as a healthy part of our life and the skills to make it a constructive experience.

5. The goal of reconciliation is to heal the relationship.

The entire purpose of working through conflict is aimed at bringing back together what has been torn apart through earlier actions, behaviors, and responses. The primary goal is reconciliation, understood as relationship and restoration, the healing of personal and social fabrics. In this process, it is impossible to separate personal from social healing.

Clearly, these are like steps in a journey. It begins with a personal journey within, for the purpose of identifying the source of pain, what is wrong, and understanding it. The process then moves us toward the source of our anxiety and the pain that is welling up in the relationship. What rises from this journey is commitment to relationship and interdependence. Reconciliation can be understood in terms of relationship, not in terms of vague, ambiguous, and merely mental processes. Restoration is understood not as going back to what was, but rather as the image of healing, making a balance, and bringing about what should be. It provides space for growth based on Truth and accountability. In this way, reconciliation is both a process and an outcome.

6. God is present.

In Matthew 18:20, Jesus says, "Where two or three are gathered in my name, I am there among them." When we recognize that Matthew 18 is dealing with conflict and working toward reconciliation, we comprehend a wholly different interpretation of this verse. "Two or three" does not refer to small numbers of gathered worshipers. It refers to those who come together to seek healing, restoration, and reconciliation. Verse 20 is a promise: where you take seriously the mission of reconciliation, I will be present with you.

GLOBAL CONFLICT: FIRST STEPS

Jer Swigart and Jon Huckins

Through our work with The Global Immersion Project, we have spent a significant amount of time among both Israelis and Palestinians as we work together to cultivate a narrative of reconciliation. As is often the case when we approach a people or place with the hopes of being or bringing the needed change, we have been the ones most changed by our friends and colleagues who reside in the Middle East. Behind so many of the subconscious stereotypes and prejudices we had acquired earlier in our lives, we began to experience the richness of friendship and fellowship among people we had previously "known" only through the latest sound bite.

As Westerners who follow Jesus, we must have a framework for understanding and engaging global conflict constructively. Geographical distance does not dismiss us from human compassion for those who are suffering. May we begin this process of compassionate and Christlike engagement and understanding. Here are some suggested starting points.

1. Grieve the loss of life.

It is easy to look at escalating death tolls as numbers that are simply a consequence of war rather than the tragic loss of precious life. Whether Israeli, Palestinian, Syrian, or Ukrainian, each is part of the human family made in the image of God. We cannot become numb to the things that should bring us to our knees. Allow yourself to feel pain on behalf of the mothers who have lost their children and the children who have lost their parents.

2. Listen, learn, and be still.

We would do well to slow down and listen to the stories of others before telling their story for them. Those who have stepped foot in other cultures—whether domestic or international—know how much we have to learn as products of each of our unique upbringings and worldviews. Slow down, listen, learn, and be still before jumping to words or actions that may do more harm than good.

3. See common humanity before political and religious differences.

We all inherently know that the diversity of humanity isn't going to allow for us all to agree perfectly on politics and religion. Rather than look at people through the lens of politics or religion, look at them through the lens of a shared humanity. All humans were made in the image of God. When we see Jesus in the eyes of the other it is much harder to hate, hurt, and demean.

4. Pray.

Pray for the healing of others, from all nations and religions. Pray for peace in places of conflict. Seek forgiveness for our blind prejudice. Ask for courage for those who promote kingdom values. Pray for new friendships to be cultivated among former enemies. Pray for your enemies.

5. Ask hard questions.

How might my political or social involvement have perpetuated or sparked damaging consequences—in thought or action? Am I an objective observer, or are there ways I can be part of the problem or part of the restoration? Is the form of Christianity, Islam, or Judaism that is being portrayed in the media an accurate form of faithful Christianity or Islam or Judaism or simply an ideological counterfeit?

6. Expand your news sources.

It's not the distance that keeps Westerners from objective news coverage; it is polarizing political, social, and financial realities that surround this region. There is no more critical time to be savvy in how you listen and learn from the media. Do not listen to only one source, but tune in to multiple sources for various perspectives. Even better, hear firsthand accounts from friends or trusted sources who are living in the place of conflict. These are complex issues that require holding multiple narratives in tension.

7. Seek out the stories of hope and reconciliation amid conflict.

There are no better instructors for the hard work of peacebuilding than those who are choosing each day to practice it in the midst of conflict. When we shift our sight from the headlines of violence and war making toward the stories of hope and reconciliation, we not only find inspiration; we find tangible instruction in how to live, love, and lead as agents of peace amid the conflicts in our own homes, neighborhoods, and cities.

8. Live a narrative of compassion.

Those of us who know and have experienced real life with the people who are now being labeled "terrorists" must bring to the table the disconnect between perception and reality. We must acquire the resources that will help us better step into this situation with eyes for common humanity, justice, and the heart of God. We must live into the narrative God desires for humanity, which inevitably leads us to care for the hurting—whether grieving families who have lost loved ones or individuals who are targets of hate and stereotyping happening in your neighborhood because of events halfway across the globe.

Jon Huckins and Jer Swigart are codirectors of The Global Immersion Project (www.globalimmerse.org), which cultivates everyday peacemakers through immersion in global conflict.

GLOBAL CONFLICT: UNDERSTANDING TERROR

John Paul Lederach

When our world changed on September 11, 2001, I was stuck in airports. Traveling between Colombia and Guatemala and eventually to the United States, I watched as the heart of America ripped, and the images flashed even in my fitful sleep. I wrote this piece in airports as I waited to get home, finally arriving a week after I had planned to return. I shared these thoughts in several venues in the days and weeks and months following September 11.

Though natural, the cry for revenge for September 11 [etc...], seemed connected to finding a way to release deep emotional anguish, a sense of powerlessness, and our collective loss. It appeared to be rooted in these social and psychological processes more than it appeared to be a plan of action to redress the injustice and prevent it from ever happening again.

I recognized that it is always easy to take potshots at our leaders from the sidelines, and to have the insights they are missing when we are not in the middle of very difficult decisions. On the other hand, having worked by that point for nearly twenty years as a mediator and proponent of nonviolent change in situations around the globe where cycles of deep violence seemed hell-bent on perpetuating themselves, and having interacted with people and movements who at the core of their identity find ways of justifying their part in the cycle, I felt responsible to try to bring ideas to the search for solutions.

I started by naming several key challenges and then asking what is the nature of a creative response that takes these seriously in the pursuit of genuine, durable, and peaceful change. Although the world has changed since I first wrote these words in 2001, I believe that the steps below still provide the scaffold for a creative response to global conflict.

1. Seek to understand the root of the anger.

The first and most important question to pose ourselves is relatively simple, though not easy to answer: How do people reach this level of anger, hatred, and frustration? From my experience, explanations that they are brainwashed by a perverted leader who holds some kind of magical power over them is an escapist simplification and will inevitably lead us to very wrongheaded responses.

Anger of this sort, what we could call generational, identity-based anger, is constructed over time through a combination of historical events, a deep sense of threat to identity, and direct experiences of sustained exclusion. This is very important to understand, because, as I will say again and again, our response to the immediate events has everything to do with whether we reinforce and provide the soil, seeds, and nutrients for future cycles of revenge and violence. Or whether we help bring change.

We should be careful to pursue one and only one thing as the strategic guidepost of our response: avoid doing what they expect. What they expect from us is the lashing out of the giant against the weak, the many against the few. This will reinforce their capacity to perpetrate the myth they carefully seek to sustain: that they are under threat, fighting an irrational and mad system that has never taken them seriously and wishes to destroy them and their people. What we need to destroy is their myth, not their people.

2. Seek to understand the nature of the organization.

Over the years of working to promote durable peace in situations of deep, sustained violence, I have discovered one consistent purpose in movements and organizations that use violence: *sustain thyself.* This is done through a number of approaches, but generally it is through decentralization of power and structure, secrecy, autonomy of action through units, and refusal to pursue the conflict on the terms of the strength and capacities of the enemy.

One of the most intriguing metaphors I have heard used in the last several years is that this enemy of the United States will be found in their holes, smoked out, and when they run and are visible, destroyed. This may work well for groundhogs, trench, and maybe even guerrilla warfare, but it is not a useful metaphor for this situation. And neither is the image that we will need to destroy the village to save it, by which the population that gives refuge to our enemies is guilty by association and therefore a legitimate target. In both instances the metaphor that guides our action misleads us because it is not connected to the reality. In more specific terms, this is not a struggle to be conceived of in geographic terms, in terms of physical spaces and places that if located can be destroyed, thereby ridding us of the problem. Quite frankly, our biggest and most visible weapon systems are mostly useless.

We need a new metaphor, and though I generally do not like medical metaphors to describe conflict, the image of a virus comes to mind because of its ability to enter unperceived, flow with a system, and harm it from within. The enemy is not located in a territory. It has entered our system. And you do not fight this kind of enemy by shooting at it. You respond by strengthening the capacity of the system to prevent the virus and strengthen its immunity. We must change metaphors and move beyond the reaction that we can duke it out with the bad guy, or we run the very serious risk of creating the environment that sustains and reproduces the virus we wish to prevent.

3. Remember that realities are constructed.

Conflict is, among other things, the process of building and sustaining very different perceptions and interpretations of reality. This means that we have at the same time multiple realities defined as such by those in conflict. In the aftermath of such horrific and unmerited violence that we have just experienced, this may sound esoteric. But we must remember that this fundamental process is how we end up referring to people as fanatics, madmen, and irrational. In the process of name-calling, we lose the critical capacity to understand that from within the ways they construct their views, it is not mad lunacy or fanaticism. All things fall together and make sense. When this is connected to a long string of actual experiences wherein their views of the facts are reinforced (for example, years of superpower struggle that used or excluded them, encroaching Western values of what is considered immoral by their religious interpretation, or the construction of an enemy-image who is overwhelmingly powerful and uses that power in bombing campaigns and always appears to win) then it is not a difficult process to construct a rational world view of heroic struggle against evil. Just as we do it, so do they.

Listen to the words we use to justify our actions and responses. And then listen to words they use. The way to break such a process is not through a frame of reference of who will win or who is stronger. In fact the inverse is true. Whoever loses, whether tactical battles or the "war" itself, finds intrinsic in the loss the seeds that give birth to the justification for renewed battle. The way to break such a cycle of justified violence is to step outside of it. This starts with understanding that TV sound bites about madmen and evil are not good sources of policy. The most significant impact that we could make on their ability to sustain their view of us as evil is to change their perception of who we are by choosing to strategically respond in unexpected ways. This will take enormous courage and courageous leadership capable of envisioning a horizon of change.

4. Understand the capacity for recruitment.

The greatest power that terror has is the ability to regenerate itself. What we most need to understand about the nature of this conflict and the change process toward a more peaceful world is how recruitment into these activities happens. In all my experiences in deep-rooted conflict, what stands out most are the ways in which political leaders wishing to end the violence believed they could achieve it by overpowering and getting rid of the perpetrator of the violence. That may have been the lesson of multiple centuries that preceded us. But it is not the lesson learned from the past thirty years. The lesson is simple. When people feel a deep sense of threat, exclusion, and generational experiences of direct violence, their greatest effort is placed on survival. Time and again in these movements, there has been an extraordinary capacity for the regeneration of chosen myths and renewed struggle.

One aspect of current U.S. leadership that coherently matches with the lessons of the past thirty years of protracted conflict settings is the statement that this will be a long struggle. What is missed is that the emphasis should be placed on removing the channels, justifications, and sources that attract and sustain recruitment into the activities. What I find extraordinary about the September 11 events is that none of the perpetrators was much older than forty and many were half that age.

This is the reality we face: recruitment happens on a sustained basis. It will not stop with the use of military force; in fact, open warfare will create the soils in which it is fed and grows. Military action to destroy terror, particularly as it affects significant and already vulnerable civilian populations, will be like hitting a fully mature dandelion with a golf club. We will participate in making sure the myth of why we are evil is sustained and we will assure yet another generation of recruits.

5. Recognize complexity but understand the power of simplicity.

Finally, we must understand the principle of simplicity. I talk a lot with my students about the need to look carefully at complexity, which is equally true (and which in the earlier points I start to explore). However, the key in our current situation that we have failed to fully comprehend is simplicity. From the standpoint of the perpetrators, the effectiveness of their actions was in finding simple ways to use the system to undo it. I believe our greatest task is to find equally creative and simple tools on the other side.

WORSHIP RESOURCES

PRAYERS

Holy One, Creator of Life:

yours is the peace that passes all understanding.

Whether the war is between countries, belief systems, varied
upbringing, family members, or churches,

finding common ground is one way to start.

For all who are searching, may your peace release hope.

For all who are aching, may your peace bring relief.

For all who are arguing, may your peace intercede.

For all who are hating, may your peace cast out fear.

May your love surround and envelop all who are

living with war, all who have been devastated by

war, and all who are perpetuating war.

May your transforming love pervade the darkness.

Amen.

—*Wilma Harder*

God of love and mercy,

Our world and our work are yours.

We are yours.

Without you we can do nothing.

God, we thank you and bless you for your own Jesus Christ

Whom you gave to the world so that all might know you more fully;

This Jesus who humbled himself in your service

To show us how to live and to love as your servants;

This Jesus who suffered and died at the hands of the powers and people

Willing to commit the great sin of violence

And violate what it means to be created in your image.

We thank you and bless you for the gift of life and love.

We thank you and bless you for all who wage peace rather than wage war.

Make us your people of peace in all that we are and do.

And now may God bless you and keep you listening and living in deepest faith;

May God's face shine upon you and bring you great joy;

And may God look upon you with favor

And keep you in the deep peace of the living Christ.

Amen. Go in peace to love and serve God.

—*Weldon Nisly*

Dear God,

You are the Word who spoke the world into being.

Be the Lord of our words on earth, as in heaven.

Give us big words and little words,

Far-reaching, wide words,

Focused words,

Truthful words that speak your peace

To our neighbors and nations.

Dear God,

You are the way, the truth, and the life through Jesus.

Be the guide for those who stand in the way today.

Stand beside

Widows and orphans,

Immigrants and refugees,

Tired and lonely ones, forgotten and dying ones,

All over your world.

Dear God,

You are our daily bread and life-giving water.

Thank you that you nourish and refresh us each day.

You strengthen our will and soften our hearts

To act justly,

To love mercy,

And to walk humbly with you, God.

To you be the glory forever, Amen.

—*Cindy Snider*

O God,
for too long the world
has called us to war,
and our dead lie sprawled
across the bleeding centuries.
But you
break the bow and shatter the spear,
calling us to sow the seeds of peace
in the midst of despair.
In tenderness,
may we take the tiniest sprouts
and plant them
where they can safely grow
into blossoms of hope.
Amen.

—*Linea Reimer Geiser*

DRAMA BASED ON PSALM 85

John Paul Lederach

> **Note:** *This skit is based on Psalm 85. See chapter 6 for more reflection on this passage. Over the years I have repeated versions of the following exercise with many different people and contexts. It varies each time. Unique and amazingly various insights emerge from people's experiences and concerns. Here is a condensed version of the exercise that I describe in chapter 6 that can be used as a short drama, especially in groups that are experiencing conflict.*

Characters:

Convener (woman or man)
Truth (woman)
Mercy (man)
Justice (man)
Peace (woman)

[*Convener walks onto a stage on which there are five empty stools or chairs. Convener sits down on one of them.*]

Convener: We have all experienced conflict and the ways that people in conflict often appeal to truth, mercy, justice, and peace. Psalm 85:10 tells us: "Mercy and Truth have met each other. Justice and Peace have kissed." So I've done some thinking, and I wondered this: What if we invited our four friends—Truth, Mercy, Justice, and Peace—to join us? What if we asked them to openly discuss their views about conflict? [*Pause.*] I have seen them come and go in other fights. So I have invited them to come and clear up a few things.

[*Truth, Mercy, Justice, and Peace enter and sit down on stools. Each wears a sign indicating who they are.*]

Convener: Welcome [*acknowledging each and shaking hands*]. We want to know what concerns you each have in the midst of conflict. May we hear your views? Truth, how about you first?

Truth [*standing*]: I am Truth. I am like light that is cast so all may see. In times of conflict, I want to bring forward what *really* happened, putting it out in the open. I am set apart from my three colleagues here [*gestures toward Mercy, Justice, and Peace*], because they need me first and foremost. Without me, they cannot go forward. When I am found, I set people free.

Convener: Sister Truth, you know I have been around a lot of conflict. There's one thing I'm always curious about. When I talk to one side, like these people over here, they say that you are with them. When I talk to the others, like our friends over there, they claim you are on *their* side. Is there only one Truth?

Truth: There is only one Truth, but I can be experienced in many different ways. I reside within each person, yet nobody owns me.

Convener: If discovering you is so crucial, why are you so hard to find?

Truth [*thoughtfully*]: I can only appear where the search is genuine and authentic. I come forward only when each person shares with others what they know of me, and when each one respects the others' voices.

Convener: Of these three friends [*pointing to Mercy, Justice, and Peace*], whom do you fear the most?

Truth [*pointing to Mercy*]: I fear him. In his haste to heal, he covers my light and clouds my clarity. He forgets that Forgiveness is *our* child, not his alone. [*Sits down.*]

Convener [*turning to Mercy*]: I am sure you have things to say. What concerns you?

Mercy [*rising slowly*]: I am Mercy. I am the new beginning. I am concerned with people and their relationships. Acceptance, compassion, and support stand with me. I know the frailty of the human condition. Who among them is perfect? [*Turns to Truth and addresses her.*] She knows that her light can bring clarity, but too often it blinds and burns. What freedom is there without life and relationship? Forgiveness is indeed our child, but not when people are arrogantly clubbed into humiliation and agony with their imperfections and weaknesses. Our child Forgiveness was birthed to provide healing.

Convener: But Brother Mercy, in your rush to accept, support, and move ahead, do you not abort the child, Forgiveness?

Mercy: I do not cover Truth's light. You must understand. I am Mercy. I am built of steadfast love that supports life itself.

Convener: And whom do you fear the most?

Mercy [*turning toward Justice and saying in a loud voice*]: My Brother Justice, in his haste to change and make things right, forgets that his roots lie in real people and relationships. [*Sits down.*]

Convener: So, Brother Justice: what do you have to say?

Justice [*rising to feet and smiling*]: I am Justice. Mercy is correct: I am concerned about making things right. I look beneath the surface and behind the issues about which people seem to fight. The roots of most conflicts are tangled in inequality, greed, and wrongdoing.

I stand with Truth, who sheds her light to expose the paths of wrongdoing. My task is to make sure that something is done to repair the damage wreaked, especially on the victims and the downtrodden.

Convener: But Brother Justice, everybody in this room feels they have been wronged. Most are willing to justify their actions, even violent deeds, as doing your bidding. Is this not true?

Justice: It is indeed. Most do not understand. [*Pauses and thinks for a moment.*] You see, I am most concerned about accountability. Often we think that anything and everything is acceptable. True and committed relationships have honest accounting and steadfast love. Love without accountability is nothing but words; love *with* accountability is changed behavior and action. My purpose is to bring action and accountability to the words.

Convener: Then whom do you fear?

Justice [*chuckling*]: My children. I fear that my children, Mercy and Peace, see themselves as parents. Yet they are actually the fruit of my labor.

Peace [*smiling and stepping forward*]: I am Peace, and I agree with all three. I am the child to whom they give birth, the mother who labors to give them life, and the spouse who accompanies them on the way. I hold the community together, with the encouragement of security, respect, and well-being.

Truth [*in a frustrated voice*]: That is precisely the problem. You see yourself as greater and bigger than the rest of us.

Justice [*chiming in, also frustrated, and pointing finger at Peace*]: Arrogance! You do not place yourself where you belong. You follow us. You do not precede us.

Peace [*softly*]: That is true, Brother Justice and Sister Truth. I am more fully expressed through and after you both. But it is also true that without me, there is no space cleared for Truth to be heard. [*Turns toward Justice.*] And without me, there is no way to break out of the vicious cycle of accusation, bitterness, and bloodshed. You yourself, Justice, cannot be fully embodied without my presence. I am before and after. There is no other way to reach me. I myself am the way.

Convener [*after moment of silence*]: And whom do you fear?

Peace: Not whom, but what and when. I fear manipulation. I fear the manipulation of people using Sister Truth for their own purposes. Some ignore her, some use her as a whip, some claim to own her. I fear times when Brother Justice is sacrificed for the sake of Brother Mercy. I fear the blind manipulation when some will sacrifice life itself in trying to reach the ideal of Brother Justice. When such trickery takes place, I am violated and left as an empty shell.

Convener [*gesturing to all of them*]: How would it be possible for you four to meet? What would you need from each other?

[*As the four characters say these next few lines, they begin moving toward each other slowly, meeting in the middle of the stage.*]

Truth [*speaking to Mercy*]: You must slow down, Brother Mercy. Give me a chance to emerge. Our child cannot be born without the slow development in the womb of the mother.

Mercy [*nodding*]: Shine bright, dear Sister Truth. But please take care not to blind and burn. Remember that each person is a child of God. Each is weak and needs support to grow.

Justice: I have been partly reassured by the words of Sister Peace. I need a clear statement that she gives a place for accountability and action. Remember when Micah spoke of us: "Love Mercy and do Justice." You, Sister Peace, must allow room for me to come forward.

Peace: Brother Justice, we need one another. Don't fall into bitterness that rages without purpose. I will provide the soil for you to work and bear fruit.

[*By now, the four are gathered in a small circle toward the center of the stage. They look at each other with a measure of surprise but also satisfaction.*]

Convener: And what is this place called where you stand together?

Truth, Mercy, Justice, and Peace [*in unison and joining hands*]: This place is called *reconciliation*.

RESOURCES FOR FURTHER STUDY ON CONFLICT AND RECONCILIATION

Sue Park-Hur, Hyun Hur, and André Gingerich Stoner

BIBLICAL AND THEOLOGICAL BASIS OF PEACEMAKING AND RECONCILIATION

Augsburger, Myron S. *The Robe of God: Reconciliation, the Believers' Church Essential.* Scottdale, PA: Herald Press, 2000.

Katongole, Emmanuel and Chris Rice. *Reconciling All Things: A Christian Vision for Justice, Peace, and Healing.* Downers Grove, IL: InterVarsity Press, 2008.

Kraybill, Donald B. *The Upside-Down Kingdom.* 5th ed. Scottdale, PA: Herald Press, 2011.

Kreider, Alan, Eleanor Kreider, and Paulus Widjaaja. *A Culture of Peace: God's Vision for the Church.* Intercourse, PA: Good Books, 2005.

Ott, Bernhard. *God's Shalom Project.* Intercourse, PA: Good Books, 2005.

Swartley, Willard M. *Slavery, Sabbath, War and Women.* Scottdale, PA: Herald Press, 1983.

Trocme, Andre. *Jesus and the Nonviolent Revolution.* Maryknoll, NY: Orbis, 2004.

Wink, Walter. *The Powers That Be.* Reprint ed. New York: Harmony, 1999.

Yoder, John Howard. *The Politics of Jesus.* 2nd ed. Grand Rapids, MI: Eerdmans, 1994.

Yoder, Perry B. *Shalom: The Bible's Word for Salvation, Justice and Peace.* Nappanee, IN: Evangel, 1998.

PACIFISM, JUST WAR, AND JUST PEACEMAKING

Barrett, Lois. *The Way God Fights: War and Peace in the Old Testament.* Scottdale, PA: Herald Press, 1987.

Driver, John. *How Christians Made Peace with War: Early Christian Understandings of War.* Eugene, OR: Wipf & Stock, 2007.

Eller, Vernard. *War and Peace: From Genesis to Revelation.* Reissue ed. Eugene: Wipf & Stock, 2003.

Roth, John. *Choosing against War: A Christian View.* Intercourse, PA: Good Books, 2002.

Stassen, Glen, ed. *Just Peacemaking: Ten Practices for Abolishing War.* Cleveland: The Pilgrim Press, 1998.

Swartley, Willard M. *Violence Renounced.* Telford, PA: Pandora, 2000.

Yoder, John Howard. *What Would You Do?* Rev. ed. Scottdale, PA: Herald Press, 1992.

———. *When War Is Unjust: Being Honest in Just-War Thinking.* 2nd ed. Eugene, OR: Wipf & Stock, 2001.

PRACTICAL PEACEMAKING

Daily Living

Sande, Ken. *Resolving Everyday Conflict.* Grand Rapids, MI: Baker Books, 2011.

Slattery, Laura, Ken Butigan, Veronica Pelicaric, and Ken Preston-Pile. *Engage: Exploring Nonviolent Living.* Long Beach, CA: Pace e Bene Press, 2005.

Vanier, Jean. *Finding Peace.* Toronto: House of Anansi, 2003.

Conflict Transformation and Mediation

Claassen, Roxanne and Ron Claassen. *Making Things Right: 32 Activities Teach Conflict Resolution and Mediation Skills.* Fresno, CA: Center for Peacemaking and Conflict Studies, Fresno Pacific University, 1987.

Lederach, John Paul. *The Little Book of Conflict Transformation.* Intercourse, PA: Good Books, 2003.

Schrock-Shenk, Carolyn and Lawrence Ressler. *Making Peace with Conflict: Practical Skills for Conflict Transformation.* Scottdale, PA: Herald Press, 1999.

Restorative Justice

Marshall, Christopher D. *Beyond Retribution: A New Testament Vision for Justice, Crime, and Punishment.* Grand Rapids, MI: Eerdmans, 2001.

Myers, Ched and Elaine Enns. *Diverse Christian Practices of Restorative Justice and Peacemaking.* Maryknoll, NY: Orbis, 2009.

———. *New Testament Reflection on Restorative Justice and Peacemaking.* Maryknoll, NY: Orbis, 2009.

Van Ness, Daniel and Karen Heetderks Strong. *Restoring Justice: An Introduction to Restorative Justice.* 5th ed. Cincinnati, OH: Anderson Publishing, 2014.

Zehr, Howard. *Changing Lenses: A New Focus for Crime and Justice.* 3rd ed. Harrisonburg, VA: Herald Press, 2005.

BIOGRAPHIES OF CHRISTIAN PEACEMAKERS

Gbowee, Leymah. *Mighty Be Our Powers: How Sisterhood, Prayer, and Sex Changed a Nation at War.* New York: Beast Books, 2011.

King, Martin Luther. *Strength to Love.* Gift ed. Minneapolis: Fortress Press, 2010.

Larson, Jonathan B. *Making Friends among the Taliban.* Harrisonburg, VA: Herald Press, 2012.

Mandela, Nelson. *Long Walk to Freedom: The Autobiography of Nelson Mandela.* New York: Back Bay Books, 1995.

Mehl-Laituri, Logan. *For God and Country (In That Order): Faith and Service for Ordinary Radicals.* Harrisonburg, VA: Herald Press, 2013.

Mosley, Don and Joyce Hollyday. *Faith Beyond Borders: Doing Justice in a Dangerous World.* Nashville: Abingdon, 2010.

Perkins, John. *Let Justice Roll Down.* Ventura, CA: Regal, 2012.

SELECTED LIST OF JOHN PAUL LEDERACH'S BOOKS

Lederach, John Paul. *Preparing for Peace: Conflict Transformation Across Cultures.* Syracuse, NY: Syracuse University Press, 1995.

———. *Building Peace: Sustainable Reconciliation in Divided Societies.* Washington, D.C.: United States Institute of Peace Press, 1997.

——— and Cynthia Sampson, eds. *From The Ground Up: Mennonite Contributions to International Peacebuilding.* Oxford, England: Oxford University Press, 2000.

——— and Jan Moomaw Jenner, eds. *Into the Eye of the Storm: A Handbook of International Peacebuilding.* San Francisco: Jossey-Bass, 2002.

———. *The Little Book of Conflict Transformation.* Intercourse, PA: Good Books, 2003.

———. *The Moral Imagination: The Art and Soul of Building Peace.* New York: Oxford University Press, 2005.

——— and Angela Jill Lederach. *When Blood and Bones Cry Out: Journeys Through the Soundscape of Healing and Reconciliation.* Santa Lucia, Queensland: University of Queensland Press, 2010; New York: Oxford University Press, 2011.

———. *The Poetic Unfolding of the Human Spirit.* Kalamazoo, MI: The Fetzer Institute, 2011.

FILMS

A Force More Powerful (2000) is a series on six nonviolent social change movements that overcame oppression and authoritarian rule. The 25-minute segment on the Nashville sit-in movement is particularly potent. http://www.aforcemore powerful.org/films/index.php

As We Forgive (2010) is a powerful documentary about two Rwandan women coming face-to-face with the men who slaughtered their families during the 1994 genocide. Can reconciliation be found? http://asweforgivemovie.com/

Bringing Down a Dictator (2002) documents the spectacular defeat of Slobodan Milosevic in October 2000, not by force of arms, as many had predicted, but by an ingenious nonviolent strategy of honest elections and massive civil disobedience. http://www.aforcemorepowerful.org

Fambul Tok (2011) documents how the victims and perpetrators of Sierra Leone's brutal civil war come together in an unprecedented program of tradition-based truth-telling and forgiveness ceremonies. http://www.fambultok.com/

Memory of Forgotten War (2013) explores the human costs of military conflict through deeply personal accounts of the Korean War by four Korean-American survivors. http://www.mufilms.org/

The Power of Forgiveness (2007) compiles stories of the Amish, Ground Zero, Thich Nhat Hanh, Elie Wiesel, and others, with reflections from Thomas Moore, James Forbes, and Marianne Williamson. http://www.thepowerofforgiveness.com

Waging Peace (2011) examines the streams of peace that flow through both the Christian and Muslim worlds by telling dramatic, challenging stories of Muslims and Christians finding peaceful solutions to conflicts. http://www.thirdway.com/peace/?Topic=360_Waging+Peace

Women, War, and Peace (2011) focuses on women's strategic role in the post–Cold War era, where globalization, arms trafficking, and illicit trade have intersected to create a whole new type of war. http://www.pbs.org/wnet/women-war-and-peace/

CHRISTIAN PEACE-RELATED ORGANIZATIONS AND COMMUNITIES

Alternatives to Violence Project: http://www.avpinternational.org

Bartimaeus Cooperative Ministries: http://bcm-net.org

Bruderhof Community: www.bruderhof.org

Christian Peacemaker Teams: www.cpt.org

Duke Center for Reconciliation: http://divinity.duke.edu/ initiatives-centers/center-reconciliation

Eastern Mennonite University Center for Justice and Peacemaking: http://www.emu.edu/cjp/

Emerging Voices Project: http://emergingvoicesproject.org/

International Justice Mission: www.ijm.org

Jubilee Partners: www.jubileepartners.org

Kairos Palestine: www.kairospalestine.ps

Koinonia Partners: www.koinoniapartners.org

Kroc Institute for International Peace Studies: http://kroc .nd.edu/

Lombard Mennonite Peace Center: http://www.lmpeacecenter .org/

Mennonite Central Committee: www.mcc.org

Northeast Asia Regional Peacebuilding Institute: www.narpi.net

Peace & Justice Support Network, Mennonite Church USA: www.pjsn.org

Reba Place Fellowship and Church: www.rebaplacefellowship.org

ReconciliAsian: www.reconciliasian.com

Sojourners: www.sojo.net

The Global Immersion Project: www.globalimmerse.org

The Simple Way: www.thesimpleway.org

Workshop: www.workshop.org.uk

Sue and Hyun Hur are codirectors of ReconciliAsian (www.reconciliasian
.com), a peace center that promotes a culture of peacemaking in Korean
and Asian immigrant churches. They are also copastors of Mountain
View Mennonite Church.

André Gingerich Stoner is director of interchurch relations and holistic
witness for Mennonite Church USA.

INVITATIONS TO ACTION

Jon Huckins and Jer Swigart

CHAPTER 1: THE THREAT TO MY ONLY CHILD

Dreaming

- Identify what is broken—in your home, neighborhood, vocational space, region, nation, country, or world—which God has given you a dream to see restored.

- Invite those you trust to help you name and refine the dream.

- Discover the influencers (in the faith, business, political, educational, or nonprofit realms) in your direct context who have dared to dream the same impossible dream.

- Discover how these influencers have turned "dreams into deeds," and collaborate with them toward your shared dream becoming reality.

Enemies

- Identify the person or the group that you would categorize as "enemy."

- Write down the biases, opinions, stories, and fears that define your "truth" about your enemy. Write down the questions you would ask your enemy if you had the opportunity.

- Humbly enter the sacred spaces of your enemy, such as important historical locations, places of worship, or places of deep pain.

- Hear the stories of your enemy through books, documentaries, podcasts, or presentations, or participate in a dialogue session that puts you in the same room with your enemies.

- Return to your list of biases, opinions, stories, and fears. Identify the new truths that are emerging for you.

CHAPTER 2: TURNING TOWARD THE FACE OF GOD: JACOB AND ESAU

Assigning dignity

- Practice the art of *virtuous gossip*: Refuse to speak ill of others. Instead, speak only of the virtue of others. Start with one day at a time and see if this doesn't become a habit. Pay attention to how God shifts your perspective and adjusts your "truth" about the other through this practice.

- Make a commitment to look every person that you encounter today in the eye (spouse, children, barista, homeless neighbors, colleagues, etc.) and pay attention to what this practice shifts in you.

Reconciliation as journey

- Identify where you are currently in the Jacob and Esau conflict paradigm with another person or group: the Move Away, the Turn Toward, the Meeting, or the Embrace.

- Envision what the Embrace, as well as what life beyond the Embrace, could look like. Write it down.

- Begin the Turn Toward by acknowledging your own contribution to the conflict.

- Pursue reconciling conversations with humility and curiosity, leading with a desire to understand rather than to be understood.

- Where forgiveness is needed, be the first to ask for it. Where forgiveness must be given, do so graciously. Where reconciliation seems impossible, seek mediation.

- After the Embrace, create healthy channels of communication and engage a healthy pace of contact in an effort to galvanize the relationship.

CHAPTER 3: THE RECONCILIATION ARTS: JESUS

The art of presence

- Status, ethnic identity, religious identity, and socioeconomic standing: identify which of these most interrupts your ability to notice another human being. Make it a point to have a personal, human encounter with someone of a different status, ethnic or religious identity, and socioeconomic standing today. Pay attention to what shifts in you as you do.

- Identify what most distracts you from being present—such as computer, smartphone, overcommitment—and establish a practice of intentional denial around it. (For example, turn off your computer or phone at eight o'clock in the evening and then back on at eight o'clock in the morning; say no to extracurricular commitments for one week.) Pay attention to the challenge of the denial and the beauty of being present.

- Establish a weekly rhythm of a prayer walk around your neighborhood. Pay attention to what is beautiful and to what is broken. Ask God to help you see what God needs you to see.

The art of reflection and self-care

- Establish a daily rhythm of solitude, stillness, and silence in which you can listen for the answer to these three questions:

  1. *God, how do you see me today?*

  2. *Jesus, how are you getting my attention right now?*

  3. *Spirit, how will I join you in what you are doing today?*

The art of accompaniment

- Share your table with someone of different perceived status, ethnic or religious identity, or socioeconomic standing than you. Invite them to bring a favorite recipe to contribute to the dinner. Practice humble curiosity and be careful not to position yourself in the place of power. Allow yourself to discover and to be delighted by the image of God in them.

- Invite a colleague with whom you frequently sit and meet to walk with you instead. Invite a neighbor, family member, or friend with whom you frequently sit to walk the neighborhood with you. Compare and contrast the experience.

CHAPTER 4: IN THE BEGINNING WAS CONFLICT: CREATION

- *Individual practice:* Enter into a practice of repentance, asking God this question: What do I need to repent of so that I can better see your image in others more clearly? Do you need to repent of your personal sense of importance? Your personal biases, opinions, and prejudices that have been ingrained through upbringing and media? Your busyness? Pay attention to the whisper of the Spirit and live what you hear the Spirit say.

- *Small group practice:* Rather than showing up and serving at a local soup kitchen or halfway house, set up a series of round-table conversations between your small group and the community that you're seeking to serve. Learn their stories, hear their pain, understand their plight, and celebrate their successes. In so doing, discover their humanity, their dignity, and the image of God within them.

- *Community-wide practice:* Invite a local Muslim imam and Jewish rabbi to a gathering where, instead of emphasizing the differences between us, you explore and highlight the common ground that we share as the three monotheistic traditions. In anticipation of this gathering, invite a working group of individuals from each community to imagine ways in which you all can walk your common ground together for the benefit of your context. As a working group, come up with one shared project and offer invitations to your faith communities to practically walk the common ground together.

CHAPTER 5: WHEN CONFLICT BURNS AND WE CRY FOR HELP: THE PSALMS

- On a piece of paper, construct a description of your enemy based on what you actually think about them by answering the following questions as raw and honestly as possible:

  1. What motivates your enemies?

  2. What are their passions?

  3. What is the objective of their behavior?

  4. What do you despise most about them?

  5. What are the main differences between you and them?

6. What kind of father/mother, brother/sister, husband/wife, and friend are they?

7. What positive contribution do they make to society?

- Second, take an honest assessment of the narrative description you've constructed.

   1. Identify how you have separated yourself from your enemy by making them everything you are not.

   2. Identify how you have placed yourself as superior (not different from, but better than) your enemy.

   3. Identify where you have deprived your enemy of qualities that make them human.

- Third, invite your enemy (or a representative of your enemy) to coffee. Rather than seeking to resolve conflict or to be understood yourself, seek to understand their story, pain, and perspective. If it's helpful, use the questions from step 1. Write down what you learn and, when alone, compare your notes. Pay attention to the differences between the two narrative descriptions.

CHAPTER 6: TRUTH, MERCY, JUSTICE, AND PEACE: PSALM 85

- With a trusted friend with whom you've experienced reconciled conflict, walk through the Truth, Mercy, Justice, Peace encounter that Lederach offers. Begin by revisiting the conflict that emerged and has been worked through. Ask each other the following:

   Truth: What really happened and how did you experience the impact of it?

Mercy: How did what happened affect your understanding of me (intent, values, etc.)? What stories about me crept into your imagination? How did these stories interrupt our relationship?

Justice: While we were still unreconciled, what did "justice" look like from your perspective? What was the justice that you longed for?

Peace: What decision did you make that broke you out of the vicious cycle of victimizing yourself and dehumanizing me?

CHAPTER 7: WHERE TWO OR THREE MEET: MATTHEW 18

Communal process for reconciliation

- **For pastors and leaders:** First, with your community of elders, take an honest assessment of how you've done in handling conflict: between parishioners, between parishioners and leadership, and between leadership with leadership. How prevalent is triangulation? Is vulnerability and taking personal responsibility common? How would you grade yourselves in your ability to work toward restoration? Can you articulate a clear process that you currently engage? Second, with the resources of Matthew 18 and chapter 7, co-create a process for navigating conflict transformationally that could become the process for you as well as for the people and families that make up the community you lead.

- **For all of us:** Consider an unresolved conflict that you find yourself in. On a piece of paper, reflect on these four questions and share your reflections with a mentor, pastor, or trusted friend who will encourage you toward reconciliation:

Self-awareness: What about myself is this conflict exposing to me that I like and dislike?

Triangulation: With whom, other than the one(s) I'm in conflict with, have I talked about this conflict? Assess: Did the conversation inspire me toward reconciliation or did it further justify my posture and deepen the conflict?

Passive aggressive: How have I tried to deal with this conflict passive aggressively?

Rightness: Why is it so important to me to be "right" about this?

Contribution: How have I contributed to the conflict and/or its longevity?

CHAPTER 8: KEEP SILENT AND LISTEN: ACTS 15

- First, with your faith community, a small group, or a trusted group of friends, do your best to identify what's most broken in your city or neighborhood.

- Second, do some research to determine which people groups are most affected by the brokenness, as well as which influencers and organizations are seeking their restoration.

- Third, invite a diverse community of men and women that is representative of those affected by and invested in the issue to a time of listening and learning.

- Fourth, as a community, host these people well by cultivating a safe environment for listening and learning. Invite those whom you've invited to help you and each other:

    1. Define and understand the problem: What are the root causes? Who are the peoples impacted and what does the impact look/feel like? What has been the impact of

historical attempts to solve the problem? Whenever diverse, foreign, or differing perspectives and experiences of the problem emerge, create space for curiosity so that a more holistic understanding can emerge.

2. Host a galvanizing dialogue around the following question: What are the steps that we, together, can take in the next ten days, ten weeks, and ten months to seek the restoration of what is broken? Set up a series of follow-up conversations around the same time frames to continue the learning and collaboration.

CHAPTER 9: RECONCILIATION *IS* THE GOSPEL: PAUL'S LETTERS

- **For pastors and leaders**: In an effort to come to a shared understanding of the mission of God, host a conversation around the following questions:

1. Without looking at your Bibles (or smartphones), what is the mission of God? Another way of asking the question would be this: What did God accomplish through the life, death, and resurrection of Jesus? On a screen or large piece of paper, capture all of the responses. Pay attention to the diversity and similarities of the answers.

2. What do the primary programs of our church communicate about what the mission of God is? List out the primary programs and stated objectives of each as they are identified, as well as new definitions of the mission of God that emerge.

3. What does 2 Corinthians 5:18-20 tell us about the mission of God as well as the vocation of God's people?

4. What might need to shift in our posture and practice with one another, within our context, and within the

world so that we can better join God in the mission of reconciliation?

- **For all of us:** Identify the one issue in your personal life, in your context, or in the world that is broken and that Jesus is inviting you toward. Ask yourself this question: What steps can I take in the next ten days, ten weeks, and ten months to humbly "move toward human troubles and choose to live in the messiness"? Write down your list and share it with trusted friends. Invite them to keep you accountable to, as well as to accompany you, on this journey.

Jon Huckins and Jer Swigart are codirectors of The Global Immersion Project (www.globalimmerse.org), which cultivates everyday peacemakers through immersion in global conflict.

For discussion questions in the form of a study guide, go to www.heraldpress.com/Studygds/reconcile. *Hal Shrader,* lead pastor of Trinity Mennonite Church, Phoenix, Arizona, created the discussion questions for this study guide.

The Author

John Paul Lederach has worked in international conciliation for more than thirty years. He has developed training in conflict transformation and provided direct mediation and support services for reconciliation efforts in some of the most violently conflicted regions across five continents. Lederach has consulted with the highest-level government officials and national opposition movements in war-torn settings like Nicaragua, Somalia, Northern Ireland, Colombia, Nepal, and the Philippines.

As professor of international peacebuilding and director of the Kroc Institute for International Peace Studies at the University of Notre Dame, Lederach is the founding director of the Center for Justice and Peacebuilding at Eastern Mennonite University, Harrisonburg, Virginia. He is the author of twenty-two books and manuals and numerous academic articles and monographs on peace education, conflict transformation, and mediation training. Lederach's books have been translated into more than a dozen languages, and he is in international demand as a lecturer, consultant, and mediation trainer.

Lederach splits his time between Indiana and Colorado. He is married to Wendy S. Liechty. They are the parents of Angie and Josh.